BILLY GRAHAM:

A Mission Accomplished

BILLY

A Mission

GRAHAM:

Accomplished

BY GEORGE BURNHAM

FLEMING H. REVELL COMPANY

THIS BOOK IS dedicated to a gracious God, my wonderful family, the Billy Graham team and The Chattanooga *News-Free Press*, an unusual newspaper which sent a man half way around the world to put God on the front page. The book would not have been possible without the cooperation of all.

I wish to express my warmest appreciation to Mr. Roy McDonald, *News-Free Press* Publisher and to Mr. Everett Allen, General Manager, for their sincere cooperation and guidance in the preparation and distribution of the stories to the newspapers of America.

I would also like to express my gratitude to Mrs. Mary Mitchell, a member of The *News-Free Press* staff, who devoted long hours in doing a superb job of distributing stories to newspapers and typing the book manuscript.

GEORGE BURNHAM

Contents

CONTENTS

10

CONTENTS

Introduction

WE HAVE BEEN HUMBLED AT THE OVERWHELMING RESPONSE to our ministry both in Britain and on the Continent of Europe. It has been beyond anything we could have possibly imagined! There are five important factors that contributed to the success of our meetings.

First, the millions of people in every part of the world who prayed. Day after day we were borne on the wings of prayer; and night after night as I gave the invitation for men to surrender their lives to Christ, I felt the impact of the prayers of countless people in all walks of life.

Second, there was the power and the authority of the quoted Word of God. I found that Scripture texts became like a rapier in my hand. I became conscious that God was not using my clever phrases or illustrative material nearly so much as He was His own Word.

Third, there was the power of the Holy Spirit. If you take the supernatural element from these British and Continental meetings, little or nothing would have been accomplished. Therefore all the praise and glory must go to God. It was His doing, and it was marvelous in our eyes!

Fourth, there was the overwhelming support of the churches everywhere. Many ministers who had mental reservations concerning this particular method of evangelism cooperated in a spirit of unity and tolerance that was the amazement of people everywhere. Our meetings are church-integrated and without the support of the clergy could not possibly be held on the scale that we have witnessed.

Fifth, there was the overwhelming support of the secular and religious press. From time to time there were critical articles, to be sure, but by and large the press was sympathetic and amazingly generous. The coverage at times was phenomenal. For example, one London newspaper during our week of meetings at Wembley Stadium ran a full page every day. Two of London's newspapers printed a special edition each day. In Glasgow all the papers carried stories daily. On the Continent it was even more amazing. The meetings were front-page news in almost every city.

But by far the greatest contribution made by any single reporter was that of George Burnham of the Chattanooga *News-Free Press*. Mr. Burnham was with us during the entire tour of 1955 and reported for more than 300 daily newspapers in the United States. His articles were read by millions and as a result thousands of people kept up with the daily behind-the-scenes happenings. Not only is George Burnham an outstanding journalist, but he is also a deeply dedicated man of God. He himself has had a remarkable conversion to Christ. As I have often heard him say, he felt that his pen was guided by the same Holy Spirit that he felt was using my tongue.

It is our prayer that these chapters that have been an inspiration to millions through the secular press will be used to inspire all who read these pages.

BILLY GRAHAM

Montreat, North Carolina

BILLY GRAHAM:

A Mission Accomplished

One Little Word

The young American preacher—tall, fair, and handsome Billy Graham—was sitting out in the middle of the Atlantic Ocean with enough problems for everybody on board the liner *United States*.

Well known in America, where unprecedented crowds gathered every time he appeared, Billy was on the way to London for his first major campaign abroad. He was almost unknown by the people of Great Britain's largest city. He knew that in a city the size of London—almost twice as large as New York City in area—a preacher could get lost and rattle around in frustration, without coming close to his objective of sparking a religious awakening in the dead and dying churches.

Then the fury of Great Britain broke around his ears. A newspaperman in London, glancing at a Billy Graham publicity calendar, rose up in journalistic indignation when he noticed a line saying that socialism had done more harm to England than communism. In England, Socialists form a major political party, like the Democrats and Republicans. Headlines blared, denouncing the brash American. A member of Parliament arose on the floor and suggested that Billy be denied the right to leave the ship when it docked at Southampton.

But Billy did land. His controversial name was on the

lips of all London. The rest is history, told in unnumbered
newspaper and magazine articles—how he preached to an
estimated 1,500,000, recorded over 40,000 decisions for Jesus
Christ and saw new life return to churches in larger and
livelier congregations.

London was followed by an incredibly successful tour
of Europe. Ambassadors and ministers of every country visited said he had done more to cement good will between the
United States and foreign nations than any man in recent
years. The combined costs of all meetings, lasting over four
months, was less than one fighter plane.

Several months later Billy left the United States, this
time for a six-weeks' campaign in Glasgow, Scotland, to be
followed by eight days in London's mammoth Wembley
Stadium and then another tour of Europe. There was no talk
this time about forbidding him the right to land. Every major
city in Great Britain wanted him to come and speak.

When his ship, the French liner *Liberte*, docked at Plymouth, England, about seven o'clock in the morning, there
was a crowd of several hundred on hand to greet him. People
lined the pier and sang the old hymns of the church as he
walked down the gangplank. Scores of clergymen from the
Church of England were among the first to grip his hand.

"What a joy it is to be back," exclaimed Billy, "but I'm
surprised you got up so early in the morning to meet me."

Shortly after leaving the ship, Billy went to see Plymouth, the seaport town from which the Pilgrims sailed to
settle a new country.

"I'm a Pilgrim Father in reverse," said Billy.

Together with several members of his team, he left by
car for London, where the doubting newspapermen of a year
before turned out in numbers usually found only at interviews by royalty. He was the toast-of-the-town!

Wanting to get to Scotland as quickly as possible for a

look around, Billy took a late sleeper-train from London to Glasgow. He was surprised the next morning, shortly after daybreak, when the train pulled into a little Scottish town. A great clamor was heard outside as scores of people yelled, "We want Billy, we want Billy."

He slipped a robe over his pajamas and spoke to the people briefly from the window of his compartment.

Billy, who grew up milking cows on a farm outside Charlotte, N. C., may be the most popular "favorite son" America has ever sent abroad. He has taken a message almost 2,000 years old from the world's dustiest Book, the Bible, and touched the hearts of people everywhere he has gone.

In Great Britain and Europe, as in the United States, he commands attention and respect wherever he appears. Presidents and prime ministers invite him in for talks. Movie stars go unnoticed when he is around. At the landing in Plymouth a famous movie actor from Hollywood was aboard. Seeing all the people waiting at the dock, he made an effort to appear modest as he assumed the people were there to greet him. But he was astonished on disembarking to find that no one paid him any attention. Their greetings were focused on a preacher who talked Jesus Christ at the drop of a hat. And if a hat wasn't dropped, he would talk about Christ anyway.

On another trans-Atlantic crossing from Europe aboard the *Queen Mary*, actor Jimmy Stewart said: "I want to meet this fellow. Everyone who comes around asking for my autograph already has his name in the book." They talked for hours, and struck up a fast friendship.

Another actor on board the ship, Spencer Tracy, told about a "young brat" who had started out on the journey making life miserable for everybody. On Sunday morning the youngster wandered into the captain's church service where Billy was speaking. One of the secrets of Billy's ministry is that he speaks in a manner which can be understood by a five-year-old, but the message is interesting to an adult. He says that too many preachers preach to other preachers, instead of to the people.

The little boy, Tracy related, went to his mother after the service and said: "Mother, I understand God the way that man explained it. And I want to be a better boy."

"And that boy is different," Tracy said. "He isn't the spoiled brat who started out on this trip."

Tough Seaport

HUGE BILLBOARDS AROUND GLASGOW, ADVERTISING THE campaign of Evangelist Billy Graham, have been mutilated —grim evidence of opposition in a city described by many as the toughest seaport in the world.

A former detective-inspector, William McRae, has asked the question:

"Is Glasgow too wicked to save?"

Billy has stated that Glasgow is in greater need of prayer than London was the year before. After his campaign there, church attendance, which had been as low as five per cent of the population, increased rapidly. Leaders in London state that the majority of the results have been lasting.

But Glasgow is like another world, according to the inspector, who asked:

"I wonder if Billy Graham's advance corps—now seated

in their offices on Sauchiehall Street—have told him what to expect?

"Have they told him of the dark-cobbled streets and bleak tenements, where innocent people live in fear of gangsterism, blackmail, and murder?

"Have they shown him the crime figures for last year— 7,840 cases of housebreaking, 9,825 cases of theft, 177 people assaulted and robbed?

"Have they warned him of the task that faces him in trying to lure young hooligans and irresponsible girls from their haunts in St. Vincent Square to his salvation meetings in the Kelvin Hall?

"The great hall," he said, "no doubt will be packed for the entire six weeks." But added:

"The minority who have given Glasgow its grim name are not likely to be among them. This minority prefer the knife and knuckleduster to Christ and crusaders."

Two years ago in Glasgow there were 287 cases of unlawful violence with weapons. The hooligans emphasized their disregard for law and order with forty-seven attacks upon policemen.

The favorite weapon is a razor blade. Young toughs have the blades fixed in the bills of their caps, with only the sharp edges sticking out. They slash the caps across the faces of victims, leaving faces in ribbons. It is not their intention to kill and face a murder charge.

Inspector McRae said organized blackmail is rife in Glasgow.

"Some of the smaller trades-people," he said, "go about their business of serving customers in constant fear that the next man to come to the counter may suddenly slash them in the face with a razor."

Shops may be wrecked, businesses ruined, simply at the whim of a gang with a ruthless thirst for money.

Most victims pay up—and stay silent.

One woman was struck on the head simply because she refused to sell cigarettes to a hooligan "on tick" (credit). A fifty-year-old man was hacked in the face because he had in some way offended the gang's idea of "law." A man was robbed while selling toffee to school children.

The vast majority of Glasgow's residents are friendly and law-abiding, but like people in cities everywhere, they are indifferent and prefer to look the other way rather than get involved.

This is the kind of city that Billy Graham has entered— a young farm boy from North Carolina who faces the problems of the world with the Word of God in his hands, in his head, and in his heart.

Stamp of Approval

BILLY GRAHAM HAS BEEN ACCLAIMED BY THE PEOPLE OF Scotland and other nations around the world. But to all this praise, he has warned: "God will not share His glory with any man. Pat me on the back and you will ruin my ministry. If people talk about Billy Graham instead of Jesus Christ, then my mission will be a failure."

The little country of Scotland, with a population of about 5,000,000, has made the evangelist's name a household word, even in remote Highlands area.

In officially welcoming Billy to Glasgow, Dr. Nevile Davidson, minister of Glasgow Cathedral, said: "A man however eloquent or clever is no use unless he has a message. We all know what that message is. It is the old, old story but told in new words, in a new setting by new methods, through the medium of a strong new voice and a consecrated personality. We believe that in this mid-twentieth century God has raised up another man of personality and powerful speech to proclaim His Word without fear or favor—the message of Jesus Christ and Him crucified."

In replying to the gracious welcome, Billy recalled from the Bible the dedication of Solomon's temple when God sent fire from heaven to consume the sacrifices and show His approval of what the people had done.

Now it was dedication day in bustling Glasgow. Never before had such preparation been made for an evangelical mission. The beautiful hall called Kelvin, with a seating capacity of about 18,000, had been prepared. Prayers had gone up to God. The people had been informed by wireless, television, and the press. Said Billy Graham: "We stand and pray that by God's will the fire will fall from heaven and the wind scatter it across Scotland till the whole country is aflame. And that a great spiritual impact will be made on a world that desperately needs Christ."

Messages from all over the world poured into Glasgow prior to the opening of the campaign. They came from Formosa, South Africa, Manila, Japan, Brazil, Mexico, America, and many other countries. One special message came to Billy from President Dwight Eisenhower, a warm personal friend. He wished the evangelist every success in his mammoth undertaking.

Then came the opening of the crusade on the first day of spring. A blinding snowstorm hit Glasgow in the same hour the services were scheduled to begin. More than 3,000 persons stood in lines over a quarter of a mile long and sang hymns as they waited for tickets. The tickets were free, but necessary—otherwise 50,000 might have shown up. One woman had given her tickets away "to someone who needed them more than I did." She took her place in line to get one of the few tickets given away each night at the hall. Others were distributed in advance. Policemen with walkie-talkies directed the people.

Remarked the Rev. Tom Allan, chairman of the All-Scotland Committee, "This is a very great day. So much can happen from this."

Billy's message was simple, unemotional, and to the point. He said, "I sincerely believe that if the world returns to repentance and faith in Jesus Christ, we can have not only individual peace but world peace.

"The Communists are talking about a world revolution. I agree that the world needs a revolution, but the kind of revolution it needs is a spiritual one in which people live like Christians seven days a week instead of just on Sunday. If a spiritual awakening takes place here, it might spread throughout the world."

In his invitation at the close of the message he urged that the revolution start in the lives of the individuals as "you repent of sin and turn to Christ in simple child-like faith."

Strangely unlike the usual Scottish procedure, he asked them to walk down the aisles and "confess Christ before men unashamedly." The first two who came were women, one pink with embarrassment or excitement, the other steadfast. Both appeared serious. There was a mother leading her three children. Then came a school boy—his hair uncombed and one of his stockings around his ankles. Young well-dressed couples held hands as they came. Elderly fathers and mothers, some with tears running down their cheeks, joined in the shuffling pilgrimage.

When the reverent procession was over, 470 had taken

their stand for Christ before the platform. This was the largest number of first-night decisions in any campaign ever held by Billy.

The fire had fallen. But most of the reporters sitting at the press table missed it. They were looking for the fire, in what some said, were the hypnotic eyes of Billy Graham. The fire was in the hearts of the 470.

It took a lot of old-fashioned American courage to give an invitation to "come forward." The pressure against such a move was the heaviest he had ever experienced. Scores of ministers, friends, and members of the crusade executive committee had strongly warned against it. They said the cold, intelligent people of Scotland had never responded to such an invitation and that this would be no exception. They expressed grave concern that the lack of response would get the meeting off on the wrong foot.

"Maybe it will be proper to give an invitation later, when the people have warmed to the crusade," said leading officials.

But Billy didn't listen to the men. He listened to God! He has stated on many occasions that evangelism is not evangelism until man has made a decision.

"Why bring a man right up to the very door of heaven," he has asked, "and then refuse him the opportunity to enter?"

He asked the people to come! And they came as many churchmen sat on the platform, slightly bug-eyed, staring at the incredible happenings.

And the snow had stopped falling as the big throng moved silently out into the night, where they slushed along singing hymns on the first day of spring.

The First Cock Crow

A BEWILDERED MAN, GROPING FOR THE TRUTH, DOES SOME unusual thinking. Here are the soul-searching thoughts of a noted British intellectual leader as he listened to Evangelist Billy Graham for the first time during the All-Scotland Crusade.

It took a particular brand of courage for Noel Stevenson, chairman of the British Broadcasting Company's "Matter of Opinion" Division, to bring his thoughts out for the world to see. He said:

"Last night I heard Billy Graham. The myriad lights in wide, low Kelvin Hall shone down on thousands of men and women who must have been wondering, as I was myself, just what their motives were for being there. Was it idle curiosity? Was it a sense of inadequacy? Was it frustration at the lack of vigor in our own churches? Was it fear of the hydrogen bomb? Or was it a need to find some compelling director for life?

"I thought of the outburst of a young man in the Youth Program I chaired some weeks ago. He faced a group of industrialists and religious and civic leaders who wanted to know why modern youth was feckless.

" 'We are a lost generation because you are lost,' he accused. 'How can you guide us when you don't even know where you're going yourselves? Oh, yes, you have brains and experience—plenty of those. But you have no aims we

can seize upon as really worthwhile. You're all out for yourselves, and we don't like that.'

"No aim worthwhile. That was the thought that kept
running through my mind as I looked about me. I wasn't
being emotional about it. I had come in a mood of wariness
—tolerant, it's true, but suspicious of mass emotion, of bril-
lant organization, of American ebulience, of snap decisions
about faith.

"But the more I thought, the more I was convinced that
here was the crux of the matter. Religion means action as
well as belief: Beliefs are the tools with which nations are
made or broken. Was it because our beliefs are not being
put into practice that we were there—seeking a way to do
it? Or had our beliefs themselves gone the way of ancient
pagan fancies?

"Across the way from me three young reporters—a girl
and two men—gave me some clues. When Billy Graham
began his address with an exhortation about original sin and
the immortal soul, they sat unmoved, whispering among
themselves, giggling and pointing with an air of professional
nonchalance.

"But when he turned to the problem of the Christian
way of life they sat mute, no longer boldly challenging the
looks of others, but with eyes downcast and a sudden
realization on their faces. Slowly they raised their heads to
face the speaker above them—and they were held spell-
bound.

"If their thoughts were like mine, it was not emotion
that held them—it was the feeling that here was something
practical that could be acted upon, not a negative and
selfish aim of personal salvation through not doing wrong,
but a positive aim of peace in God through doing a thousand
small things right.

"Come to think of it, the most surprising thing about the

whole evening was the playing down of emotion. Of course
the glorious singing of the massed choir and the great
congregation warmed our hearts. Even the press—led by a
woman reporter with a voice of soft beauty—was drawn
into taking an active part. But Cliff Barrows, who led the
singing, was relaxed and cheerful. Billy Graham himself, at
a critical moment, would release the tension by raising a
smile in the name of Jesus.

"It seemed clear to me that we were being asked to
consider our position in regard to our God, and our fellow
men in the light of common sense and reason. Our love
was to be the love of happy marriage rather than of
passionate courtship; we were to keep our eyes open as well
as our hearts.

"Almost before I knew it, the climax of the evening
had arrived. Billy Graham called us to silence and to
prayer, so that those who felt called to commit their lives
to Christ might come forward and stand before the rostrum.

"In the agonized moments of hesitation that followed
I felt a rush of gratitude to see that almost all the press men
present had the grace to sit with eyes averted from this
public trial of courage and faith.

"Then the flow began, and we felt able to look about.
A young man broke from the restraining fingers of his
friends and joined the widening stream. Near me, most were
young or in early middle age—ordinary, decent young
folk—many clearly poor, others well dressed. All were quiet
and composed. I saw a sprinkling of university students
among them, and thought again of the young man in the
radio program and his cry for leadership.

"I knew in that moment that I should have been
standing there among those youngsters, giving a lead in the
public declaration of my faith.

"Panic held me when I realized that I had not the

courage of my conviction. I was thinking not of what I should do, but of how I might explain it to the intellectual critics I would have to face.

"I hesitated and was lost. That boy was right—I had failed to give a lead where one was needed.

"As the tail end of the stream flowed past and out of sight I heard, in the depths of my conscience, the first cock crow."

* * *

Facts and thoughts:

Serving with Billy Graham as associate evangelists during the All-Scotland Crusade are the Rev. Grady Wilson, a member of his regular team; Howard Butt, wealthy young businessman from Corpus Christi, Texas; and Dr. Paul Rees, noted minister from Minneapolis, Minn.

They speak daily at universities, factories, civic clubs, and other meetings apart from the regular nightly meetings at Kelvin Hall.

* * *

Crusade Quotes:

"If anybody had suggested, even a couple of years ago, that a young American evangelist would draw well over 100,000 people to a crusade in one week in Glasgow the response would have been incredulous."—Glasgow *Evening Citizen*.

A Little Child

"AND A LITTLE CHILD SHALL LEAD THEM." THERE ARE DEFINITE indications that tiny Scotland, a lively infant among ponderous giants, may be the nation which will spark civilization's spiritual awakening—a situation seen by religious and secular leaders everywhere as the only hope of a world doomed by confusion, frustration, and atomic destruction.

Sir Winston Churchill has said:

"Our problems have gotten quite beyond us. The human mind is not capable of solving the problems that face the world."

President Dwight Eisenhower has stated that a return to God is the only hope for peace.

Church leaders throughout the world have warned: "We must repent or perish."

The Bible says:

"If my people which are called by my name, shall humble themselves, and pray, and seek my face, and turn from their wicked ways, then will I hear from heaven, and will forgive their sin, and will heal their land."

Billy Graham told the writer:

"The people of Scotland are coming closer to meeting God's demands for a real religious revival than any I have ever seen. This could be the spark that will flame around the world."

The sun never sets on the prayer meetings now being held for Glasgow. People around the world, on New York's

Fifth Avenue, in the industrial boom of Detroit, in remote missionary posts of darkest Africa, are praying that God will begin a religious awakening in Glasgow that will circle the earth.

There has been no time in history when the clergy of Scotland was united in such a way, working and praying for a common goal.

In speaking of the crusade, the Rt. Rev. Ernest D. Jarvis, moderator of the General Assembly of the Church of Scotland, said:

"Certain it is that the ministers are supporting, and indeed, throwing themselves into this mission as never before in living memory.

"They are men who served in the Navy, Army, and Air Force during the war who, knowing well that it has no material prizes to offer, have entered the ministry, because they have found in Christ the answer not only to their own problems, but to the world's need.

". . . scientific achievement has somehow created a situation that is out of human control, and the country, let alone the world, is not fit for heroes, or indeed anyone else to live in."

Added the Rev. Nevile Davidson:

"Reverence for the Book is engrained in Scottish character. Still the great majority of men and women think of the Bible as the Word of God, and will listen to a man who obviously preaches with continual reference to its authority and with a passionate conviction of its truth . . . Billy Graham has been clearly raised up for a special work in our time."

During a meeting in which he addressed several hundred ministers of Scotland, Graham said:

"I live in a little town in North Carolina, which has a population of about 500. There are high mountains almost everywhere you look. Before leaving for Scotland, I went out almost every day and climbed one of these mountains, partly for the exercise, but mostly because I wanted to be alone on a mountaintop with God.

"I often fell to my knees and prayed that God would set Scotland aflame. Moments of fear and trembling came as I knelt there before God and dedicated my life all over again.

"Great floods of expectancy came into my soul and I felt strongly that the harvest was about to come in. Let us have faith to believe what God can do in Scotland.

"All the elements for revival are here. Glasgow is the most prayed-for city in the history of the Christian church. It will not be a miracle if we have revival. It will be a miracle if we don't.

"And the church must lead the way. Do you ever remember a time in history when world leaders admitted their failure and said the world was doomed unless a spiritual awakening occurred?

"I don't!"

*   *   *

Howard Butt heard reports before leaving America about the awful taste of coffee in Great Britain, where Elizabeth is Queen and tea is King.

He decided to bring along a case of one of the well-known brands from the United States, but in the process had to go through a nightmare of difficulties in mothering the precious cargo through customs.

The hardy Texan finally reached Glasgow with the coffee and enjoyed his favorite brand for several days. Then one afternoon he was having lunch in the home of some Glasgowegians and remarked on the unusually excellent taste of the coffee they served.

"What kind is it?" he asked.

His host named the brand. It was the same kind he had lugged all the way from Texas.

"You can buy it in any store here," said the Scot, as Howard quietly had an attack of coffee nerves.

* * *

Dr. Paul Rees gave this pertinent illustration:

A garrulous atheist was filling the train compartment with his profane language.

"God! God! There ain't no such being as a God," he shouted.

"That's curious," observed a quiet man in the compartment. "I happen to know Him." After a pause he added: "More curious still, you happen to hate Him."

Young at Heart

OLD PEOPLE CAN FEEL YOUNG IN HEART AGAIN THROUGH THE inspiring story of Adrian Alexander McCaskill, seventy-nine-year-old pensioner from New Orleans who provided a dramatic moment at Kelvin Hall.

A tall figure, gnarled and somewhat bent with age, Mr. McCaskill had arrived late for the meeting and was looking for a seat down front. Failing to find one in the overflow crowd, he went out and found a chair. He placed it near the platform, but an usher whispered he would have to move and was leading him down an aisle when Billy jumped from his seat and cried, in a voice which rang through the hall:

"That man—hold that man. Let him turn and face us."

An electric shock spread through the packed throng. The first thought was that someone was making trouble.

Mr. McCaskill, wearing an American Army greatcoat, stood with downcast eyes as Billy continued:

"This man comes from New Orleans, La. He is nearly eighty years of age and has followed us all over the United States. He lives on a small pension—there are very few of you here who could live on it. He saves his pennies, and ministers in New Orleans give him a few dollars to help out.

"I don't know how he got here. I didn't even know he was here. But he is here—and he has a right to a seat anywhere in this auditorium as far as I'm concerned."

The old man stood straight and tall and his eyes clouded as he looked at the young preacher who had interrupted his thoughts on a message to express appreciation for a long journey.

An usher allowed him to place the seat near the front.

After the service he was mobbed by the press and well-wishers from both sides of the Atlantic.

"God bless you, sir," said some of the people as they pressed shillings and dollars into his hand. Soon his little snap pocketbook was overflowing.

"My, I have never been so famous in all my life," he beamed.

Next day, as the luncheon guest of the writer and George Beverly Shea, soloist for the Graham team, Mr. McCaskill told about his experience.

He first heard Billy speak several years ago in San Francisco. Since that time, he has visited every American campaign conducted by the evangelist, managing it all on a sixty-five-dollar-a-month pension and the little he makes selling religious songs he has written. Some of the meetings he attended were held at Houston, Chattanooga, St. Louis, Portland, Detroit, Syracuse, and Dallas.

He dreamed of attending the first meetings in London, but this was just a little beyond his means and dreams. He continued to save the pennies, nickels, and dollars in the hope that he might come to Scotland.

Then came one of the big decisions of his life. The goal was in sight and it looked as if he could make the trip.

"But I felt very deeply that the Lord wanted me to give $100 to a foreign missions project," he said. "The old devil started talking to me and said, 'Don't be a fool; you will never get to Scotland if you give $100 of your savings away.'

"I trusted the Lord and gave it anyway. It wasn't a month I had the $100 back, and more besides."

The old man cried softly as he recalled the statement of the man who sold him his ticket for the journey: "This trip will be the fitting climax for a well-spent life."

Added Mr. McCaskill:

"Before I left New Orleans I prayed and asked God to help me witness along the way and win people for Christ. I won a man in North Carolina."

In New York City he boarded the *Italia* and on the following Sunday aboard ship he preached at the regular morning service. There were some Germans on board and whenever he had the opportunity he recited John 3:16 to them in German. He has learned the Bible's most famous verse in several languages.

On the trip across he spent fifty cents to go swimming twice.

After he had disembarked at Plymouth a little girl stuck her head out a porthole and said:

"Mister, you did a wonderful job of telling us about Jesus at the service."

Again his eyes misted as he said:

"It was worth going all the way around the world to hear a little girl say that."

A Baptist lay preacher and mission worker practically all his life, Mr. McCaskill, who has no family, expressed hope of finding some of his forebears in Scotland before he sailed for home.

"I want to help Billy as long as I am here," he said. His help consists of prayer and witnessing, two things sought more than any other by the evangelist.

"It has been wonderful getting to visit Scotland and see the people. They have so little, compared to Americans. You know, we Americans have never really appreciated our country the way we should."

As he finished the meal and pushed back in his chair, Mr. McCaskill said:

"I would like to visit Paris before going home.

"You see, I know John 3:16 in French, and that's enough to win people for Christ."

*   *   *

Crusade Items:

The Rev. Tom Allan, who has a fascinating voice like that of the late Peter Marshall, was a combatant with the RAF during World War II. At a French Protestant church, in the shadow of Rheims Cathedral, he listened to a Negro soldier sing a spiritual and was converted. Name of the spiritual was "Were You There When They Crucified My Lord?" . . . A party of 500 school children attending a Graham rally were told by their teacher "not to get saved as they had to catch a train." . . . Sob-singer Johnnny Ray, appearing at a Glasgow night club, offered to sing a hymn at a Graham meeting. Cliff Barrows expressed appreciation for the offer, but it was declined.

Brilliant Theologians

BILLY GRAHAM, WHO DIDN'T HAVE A SEMINARY EDUCATION, glanced nervously over the throng of about 1,000 distinguished Scotland ministers before he spoke:

"Every time I am called upon to address a group of ministers I become extremely nervous. The perspiration comes in the palms of my hands and the night before I have difficulty sleeping.

"This was no exception until I walked in here, sat in the chair, looked over the audience, and saw some people smiling. You looked like human beings and I relaxed.

"I was just beginning to feel good when the Rev. John Sutherland Bonnell (pastor of New York City's Fifth Avenue Presbyterian Church) leaned over and whispered, 'I seriously doubt if anywhere in the world you would gather so many brilliant men of theological turn as you have here this morning.'

"Immediately, my nervous temperment shot back up and I stand here in fear and trembling."

The tall, young evangelist, who seems to have an instinct for doing the right thing at the right time, soothed any ruffled feelings of ministers who might have objections to American evangelism methods. He said:

"Contrary to what most people in Great Britain and Europe think, all Americans are not rich. I grew up on a small farm in North Carolina and my father worked hard to provide for his family.

"Every year we would take a plough to the land. It was hard, poor soil. After it was turned over, we would harrow the dirt and work with it until it was almost as fine as powder. The crops would be planted and tenderly cared for until the time for harvest came. We found it impossible to bring in all the harvest ourselves, so my father brought in outside help. My mother cooked for all these people, and we children stood around and prayed they would leave something for us.

"Now who deserved the most credit for that crop— my father, who had done the ploughing and planting, or the harvesters who came to gather it in?

"We have come to Scotland for the same reason. We are the harvesters. You have done the work, and deserve the credit."

The evangelist asked all those ministers who held reservations against the meetings in Kelvin Hall to move their objections aside for several weeks and give the harvesters a chance to do even more.

He illustrated the point by revealing the contents of two letters he received in Glasgow about the previous meetings in London.

"The pastor of one church wrote that his congregations went all-out for the Harringay crusade. They made a house-to-house canvass of people in the parish and provided free transportation to the meetings. The pastor said that as a result the membership of his church has tripled since we left.

"The pastor of another church in London wrote that he was against the Harringay meeting from the start and wanted no part of it. The congregation did nothing. Still, in an effort to criticize the meeting at this date, he said that thirty of the people who made decisions there had listed his church as their preference. He didn't contact these thirty, and to prove his point that the decisions were not real, he said only about ten of the people ever showed up for services. In his letter he said he had taken in about two families, but was pretty sure one of these was dissatisfied. I don't wonder!

"Let's give these meetings in Glasgow a chance to show what they can do for your churches."

The evangelist reminded the ministers that "Glasgow is the most prayed-for city in the history of the Christian church," and added:

"Your responsibility is tremendous. From Scotland, more than any other place on this planet, could be launched a spiritual awakening to the entire world. If we fail in Scotland, where so much of the religious world looks for leadership, the consequences would be beyond words to describe in the discouragement that would come to the church everywhere."

He urged each minister to make a personal rededication of his life in an effort to bring about the revival "so desperately needed by the world."

Following the talk by Graham, Dr. Bonnell, a native of Scotland who has served his noted New York church since 1937, placed a few well-chosen words in the direction of the several ministers who had raised public objections to children under sixteen attending the Kelvin Hall meetings.

He stated:

"I heard one pastor make a statement to this effect the other day, and it struck me hard. I turned on him and said, 'What have you got against me, brother? I was saved as a boy of fourteen when a missionary came to our section and told us about Jesus Christ. Six months later I dedicated my life to preparation for the ministry. If I hadn't made that decision when I was fourteen, I might never have made it."

And he reminded: "Just because you are ministers doesn't mean there isn't sin and temptation in your lives. The personal devil of every preacher is jealousy, and jealousy is a sin. I know just how you feel when someone comes up

and tells you about the pastor of the church down in the next
block, what a wonderful preacher he is, and how the
people are packing in to hear him. A great glow of satisfac-
tion comes into your heart and you are so thankful for the
young preacher and his popularity."

A low chuckle rippled through the audience to show
how well Dr. Bonnell had scored.

Dr. Bonnell reminded the clergy that the theological
training was important, but that it wasn't everything. He
said:

"The last sermon that Dwight L. Moody (an edu-
cated great evangelist of many years ago) preached was in
my church on Fifth Avenue. A member of my congregation,
in telling me about it later, said he resented the mannerisms
of Moody in the pulpit and was horrified at the improper
language used—'I ain't—he don't, etc.'

"But he said that the longer Moody spoke the more
enthralled he became. He related that the hush of God
seemed to come over the congregation and that men were
visibly moved who had resisted the Holy Spirit for years."

Added Dr. Bonnell:

"Just remember, gentlemen, the foolishness of God is
wiser than men."

Flesh and Blood

OVER 3,000 PEOPLE, A COLD STATISTIC, MADE DECISIONS
surrendering their lives to Christ in the first eight days of
Billy's Scotland crusade.

But let's reduce the figure to warm flesh and blood—people with fears, frustrations, problems, and hope, much like the man-on-the-street in America.

The telephone rang in the home of one of Glasgow's leading merchants, as he and his wife were having luncheon with Billy's soloist, George Beverly Shea, his wife and son. The merchant's wife, who serves as a counselor in Kelvin Hall, was summoned to the phone.

On the other end of the line was a distraught lady with panic in her voice. She said: "You're the lady who counseled me last night after I made a decision for Christ. I want you to take the card I signed and tear it up . . . please."

Pressed for details, the lady said that both she and her daughter had "gone forward" at the service, but when they returned home later and told the husband, he was furious.

"He has threatened to leave us unless we forget all about it," said the woman. "He says he is going to the pastor where we are all members and get this thing straightened out. It isn't that we are ashamed of the decision we made, but I don't want my husband to leave. We want to talk with him about Christ. I'm afraid our pastor isn't going to like what we did either, but as Mr. Graham spoke I knew I had never surrendered my life to Christ."

The merchant's wife promised to do everything she could to help, and asked Bev Shea for advice. He told her that in a similar situation in another city, the pastor had been contacted by a friend before the father arrived and everything was settled peacefully.

A call was quickly made to the Glasgow minister and the situation explained. He listened politely and then said, "My, my, so Mrs.—— and her daughter have made decisions to live for Christ. Have no fear, dear lady, I think it's wonderful. You know, they had only been interested in the social side of church life before.

"And you tell Mrs.—— not to worry about her husband. I'll have a talk with him. Everything will be all right."

In another case, a repair man came into the Billy Graham crusade office in downtown Glasgow one morning to work on the mimeograph machine. He seemed very cynical about all the volunteer workers for Christ in the office and was scornful of all the publicity connected with the meetings.

One of the secretaries began talking with him and in the conversation told about two girls who had found Christ the night before at Kelvin Hall. He became interested in the simple, direct testimony of how two lives had been changed. The secretary asked him to do some serious thinking about his own life. He promised to try.

That afternoon at three o'clock he returned and said, "Can anybody here show me how to become a Christian?" One of the workers took him into a private room and opened a Bible. She showed him with Bible verses that he was a sinner, that Jesus Christ loved him enough to die for him, and that eternal life was his if he would surrender his will to Christ. He made the decision. Later he came into the office and asked for two tickets, saying he had two friends he wanted to take to the meeting. Both walked to the front that night when Billy gave the invitation to "accept Christ and begin living for Him seven days a week."

An engineer, who had spent most of his life in France, said he felt condemned when Billy made reference in a sermon to men in the last war who, when in great danger made vows to God, and then failed to keep them when the danger passed.

"I made a solemn vow to God once that if He would help me I would follow Him," said the engineer, "but I didn't keep it."

Both he and his wife made decisions the same night!

Crusade worker Irene Johnson spoke one night at a YWCA and remarked during the talk that she would be available for counseling afterwards if anyone wanted to see her. A total of thirteen girls came to her and made decisions.

Between sobs, a woman said she was an American citizen and had come to Scotland against the wishes of her husband and that the husband had died before she could return. "Only God can help me now," said the woman, who told of having a Christian mother living in Canada. "I'm going back to her," she murmured.

Another lady had a worried expression as she talked with a woman in the counseling room after making a decision.

"I don't know how my son will take the news about this," she said. At that moment she felt an arm being slipped around her shoulders and a voice said: "Don't worry about telling me, Mom. I came to the meeting tonight without your knowing it and I've found Christ, too."

The Queen Watches

THE WORLD'S LARGEST CONGREGATION, ESTIMATED AT 30,000,000, looked and listened on Good Friday to the "greatest love story ever told," as Billy became the first preacher in history to speak on the combined facilities of BBC and BBC-TV.

The Queen of England and members of the royal family were included in the television audience.

Several factors contributed to the incredible number of viewers and listeners. Unlike the United States, people in the British Isles either tune in on BBC or nothing. There was no choice. The newspaper strike was on in London, cutting off millions from their regular means of news. But topping off all this was the fact that the people wanted to see Billy Graham. He has captured the interest of Great Britain as have few other men in history.

The free offer by BBC came in answer to public demand. The message, transmitted in its entirety from the platform of Kelvin Hall, was centered around the death of Jesus Christ.

Billy took as his text Galatians 6:14, which reads, "But God forbid that I should glory, save in the cross of our Lord Jesus Christ, by whom the world is crucified unto me, and I unto the world."

He said, "Paul wrote to the Galatians that he gloried in the death of Jesus Christ. Why should he glory in the death of a man he worshiped? Christ died a horrible death as He hung there between heaven and earth with a spike through each hand and another through His feet. Doesn't it seem odd that Paul should glory in such an event? Paul gloried in the death of Christ because it was an expression of the depth of sin. God hates sin. It makes Him shudder. But the Bible teaches that all have sinned and come short of the glory of God. This Book says, 'There is none good, no not one.'

"Man is a sinner by nature and he is a sinner by choice. There is something inside that makes him lie, steal, cheat, and lust. Paul gloried in the cross of Christ because it describes the height of God's love to man. In 1936 the Duke of Windsor gave up the title of King of England to marry a woman of his choice and the world labeled this event the world's greatest love story. I disagree. The greatest love story ever told was the story of the death of Jesus Christ.

"God loved you so much that He let His son die in your place. The Bible says, 'For God so loved the world, that he gave his only begotten Son, that whosoever believeth in him should not perish, but have everlasting life.'

"Paul gloried in the cross because the death of Christ provided the only salvation for man. Many people think they can get to heaven by following their conscience. Their conscience may be dead. Others think they can get to heaven if they are sincere. They can be sincerely wrong. The Bible says there is a way that seemeth right unto man but the end thereof is destruction. The death of Christ provided the only way for man to get to heaven.

"I want you to get a picture of the type of people gathered around the cross while Christ died. There was Caiaphas, the high priest. His great sin was self-interest. He had to defend his dignity. The world is filled with people like that today.

"There was Pilate. His great sin was cowardice. He loved the applause of men more than he loved God. We need men of courage today who will take their stand at the cross and stand there unmovable.

"There was Herod, who loved a sensual life. There were those who hated Jesus. They whipped Jesus, hit Him with stones, and spat in His face.

"He didn't have to hang there. And if there had been any other way in the world for you to get to heaven, He wouldn't have died.

"But the biggest crowd around the cross that day was the indifferent. They couldn't care less. The Bible says that they sat down and watched. They were lukewarm. The strongest language in the Bible is reserved for this type of man. The indifferent person makes God sick at His stomach. Revelation 3:16 says, 'So then because thou art lukewarm, and neither cold nor hot, I will spue thee out of my mouth.'

"The same crowd is present in the world today. May God have mercy on them. They will be forever separated from God unless they repent of sin, accept by faith the death of Christ on the cross, and then bend their will to do the will of God."

Ministers Troubled

BILLY IS HAVING A DISTURBING EFFECT ON THE MINISTERS of Scotland!

This perhaps is the most significant thing about the crusade—well above the tremendous crowds and thousands of decisions.

A minister came to Billy and said:

"You are having a serious effect on my ministry. For years I have taught in my church that many of the stories in the Bible are myths, but I realize now that I have never had any power in my sermons. You stand there on the platform night after night and tell these same stories as the gospel truth. And I have seen with my own eyes the power of God as the people get out of their seats and walk to the front.

"Your preaching has caused me to do some very serious thinking."

A troubled mother after attending a service said that she had always regarded the story of Adam and Eve as nothing more than a fairy tale, "but I heard Billy Graham tell it as truth in describing how they sinned in the Garden

of Eden. The sermon moved me deeply and I returned home
to do some checking. I found that our school books teach
that such stories are mythical. Somebody is wrong and I
would like to know the answer."

Billy has never made any bones about the fact that
he feels the power in his ministry comes from prayer, and
preaching with conviction the Bible as the inspired Word
of God. He believes the Bible from cover to cover.

"People today," he said, "are looking for the voice of
authority. They have tried the scientist, the politician, the
philosopher. They want something on which they can stand.
The Bible is it! Jesus spoke with authority. Nowhere in the
Bible does it quote Jesus as saying 'I think so; maybe this is
the answer.' Jesus said, 'This is the way; walk ye in it.'
He said, 'I am the way, the truth, and the life: no man
cometh unto the Father, but by me.'"

Billy added:

"There is an appalling lack of reading of the Bible. We
read a great deal of criticism of the Bible, but most of the
average critics I meet have no inkling as to what the Bible
actually says. It is just hearsay; they do not read and absorb
it for themselves."

He said he had found in his own life that when he
was tempted, the greatest resource at his command was a
verse of Scripture.

"When I touch the Bible and quote its words, it is
like a rapier or a sword in my hand to win men to Christ,"
Billy said.

Bible sales in Glasgow soared after the start of the
crusade.

The Rt. Rev. E. D. Jarvis, warned there will be no new
day for religion in Scotland unless the Bible comes into its
own again and unless there is a clearer understanding of
what is meant by saying it is the Word of God.

He said:

"Too many people, both believers and unbelievers, presuppose what God's Word should be, and do not really allow the Bible to show them what it is."

Along with a return to the Bible, Dr. Jarvis said there must be a recovery of the belief in prayer. Pray regularly, he advised, not set and "pulpity" prayers, but naturally and persistently for home, friends, minister, and church.

The Rt. Rev. K. C. H. Warner, Bishop of Edinburgh of the Episcopal Church in England, also urged people to open their Bibles and find out what was inside.

In speaking of the All-Scotland Crusade, Dr. Warner said:

"Say what you like about the great meetings Mr. Billy Graham seems to be able to attract wherever he goes, the fact is that somehow and for some reason there are many thousands of people who are willing to go enormous distances to hear him.

"Is it just that they want to see this man from America, or that they have got some sort of sentimental ideas about him? I dare say that there was a good deal of curiosity about it. There was a good deal of curiosity about John the Baptist, but the people who traveled into the desert to seek him found there was a message for them.

"But surely there is something deeper than mere curiosity. This is, I believe, a symptom of a revival which is going on, an indication that there is an unexpressed feeling among people that here is a way through the tangled future."

A Glasgow newspaper conducted a survey in an effort to come up with the real Scotland verdict on Billy Graham and his Bible message. The finding:

"Billy Graham, in a way no man has done this century, has started people thinking about the church and Christianity."

Said one reader: "At last people are listening to preaching as Christ instructed His disciples to preach, so that even a little child can understand." Wrote another: "It has shaken us out of our complacency." Still a third: "My miniature Bible had not been dusted for forty years. Now it comes out every morning for a few chapters to be read. I mean to join a church." Another: "Billy Graham is very sincere, just like the old ministers of long ago. The churches used to be packed in my young days, with pews filled with families."

Fire on Heather

THERE'S FIRE ON THE HEATHER IN SCOTLAND. THIS EXPRESSION, used for years by Scots to describe unusual religious movements, is being heard throughout the country again.

Billy Graham has reached the cities, towns, and remote hamlets of the Highlands.

The most popular topic of conversation—on the streets, in night clubs, shipyards, and civic luncheons—is Jesus Christ and Billy Graham. Members of the Scotch clergy have stated that such a situation has never existed in the present generation. A vast majority of the talk is favorable, but the loud minority, always present, serves to keep the subject alive.

With modern amplification and electronics, Billy addresses most of the nation each night on a special relay system.

People gather in hundreds of halls and listen to the

services from Kelvin. Without ever seeing Billy Graham they make decisions for Christ by the thousands. Scores of Scottish pastors who had never in their ministry given an invitation for people to come forward at services are present at the relay points to give the invitations.

Long after Billy Graham has departed from Scotland these ministers will continue to give the invitation at their own churches. They have sensed the mood and hunger of the people.

Every medium of transmission has been opened to the popular American evangelist. Millions of people have been reached on radio and television.

A young millionaire in the Highland city of Inverness was stretched out on his bed on Sunday morning. Everything he touched had turned to gold. He later confided that he had everything and didn't need God. For no particular reason he reached over and flicked on the radio at the side of the bed. Billy was speaking over BBC and said, among other things, "What shall it profit a man if he gain the whole world and lose his own soul? You can take every dollar in the Bank of England and all the treasures of Europe, but God says they amount to nothing in comparison with one human soul."

The young man got out of bed and dressed. A few minutes later he walked into church and took a seat in front of his brother. The brother tapped him on the shoulder and said, "John, I'm glad to see you here. I've been praying for you a long time." The man turned and said, "You're going to see me here a lot from now on. I realized while listening to a man on the radio a little while ago how futile my life has been."

A doctor was driving from Edinburgh to Glasgow and turned on his radio. Again Billy was speaking. "Only Christ can give you eternal life, but He also provides victory over every temptation in the life you have on earth." The doctor wrote that he had been a slave to alcohol but found a whole new existence as he rode along the highway.

A converted businessman in Sussex, England, revolutionized his business with God as the senior partner. Together with his employes he begins each business day with a prayer meeting.

Scores of similar events happen throughout Great Britain every day. The Rev. Tom Allan said, "It is impossible to realize the impact this campaign has had on the life of Scottish people at every level. And the most wonderful thing about it is that people are not talking about Billy Graham. They are talking about Jesus Christ. I am convinced we are standing on the threshold of the greatest religious movement in the history of the Christian church."

On Easter Sunday Billy preached to an overflow congregation in Perth's famous St. John's Kirk (Church). It was from the same pulpit that in 1559 John Knox preached with such fervor that a riot ensued, sparking the reformation.

The traditional old church, which was founded in 500 A.D., played an important part in the national heritage of Scotland. The names of kings and queens are woven in the fabrics of its story. Edward I of England worshiped there. One of the congregation's most treasured possessions is a communal chalice reputed to be the gift of Mary of Guise, mother of Mary Queen of Scots. A beautiful baptismal basin, dated 1649, was given by Charles II. In 1644, 800 covenanters were imprisoned there by Montrose after the Battle of Tibbernuir. The Earl of Cornwall was slain before the high altar by his brother, King Edward III, in 1335.

Standing there knee-deep in history and tradition, Billy told the congregation, "You will never see the Kingdom of Heaven unless you are born again through faith in Jesus Christ." He quoted St. John 11:25-26, "Jesus said unto her, I am the resurrection, and the life: he that believeth in me, though he were dead, yet shall he live: and whosover liveth and believeth in me shall never die. Believest thou this?" And many believed.

Theological Blockbuster

A STRAPPING SIX-FOOT PLUS PREACHER FROM CALIFORNIA, pastor for twelve years of the largest Presbyterian church in the world, dropped a blockbuster among distinguished theologians of Scotland. And the debris is still falling.

Dr. Louis Evans, former pastor of the Hollywood Presbyterian Church and now minister-at-large for the Presbyterian Church USA, made a flying trip to Scotland as the guest of Billy Graham to address several hundred ministers.

In a direct attack against brilliant preachers who get all involved in theology and talk over the heads of people, he knocked a little starch out of stiff collars by stating, "We are never profound until we are clear. The average university student in America or Scotland has a third grade spiritual education. We must explain the gospel of Jesus Christ to the people step-by-step, in language they can understand.

"A Presbyterian layman told me once that he joined the church on confusion of faith. There has never been such a need for clarity. Talk straight. A little boy was writing an essay on the mystery of life. He went to his brother, father, and grandfather asking each one how they were born. Each replied, 'A stork brought me.' The little boy started off his essay, 'There hasn't been a normal birth in our family in three generations.'"

Dr. Evans warned that another great danger of the

ministry is professionalism. "Many preachers today are so wrapped up in their programs they don't have time to mingle with the people—help them and love them. They hate sin, but fail to love the people.

"A social worker and her friend were out one day and saw a mother with a filthy ragged child. The social worker asked, 'Doesn't that mother love her child?' The friend replied, 'Yes, the mother loves her child. She just doesn't happen to hate dirt.' The social worker hated dirt, but she didn't love the child."

Dr. Evans reminded the ministers that "we are not saved just to be saved. We were saved to serve. If we are His, then we are in His service. If we're not in His service, then we're not His. Unavailability is just as bad as adultery.

"Jesus Christ talked all night to Nicodemus. How long has it been since you talked all night with a man about his soul? Christ passed up His lunch to talk with a woman at the well of Samaria. How long has it been since you gave up your lunch hour to help someone? Jesus took a harlot by the hand and lifted her up. How long has it been since you proclaimed the gospel to prostitutes?"

Dr. Evans, who is the summer pastor of President Eisenhower at the National Presbyterian Church in Washington, said he was told recently by the President, "What the world needs is not more political genius but more inner integrity. God give it to me!"

In warning about smugness by a particular church denomination, Dr. Evans said, "Many churches use different ways to get devils out of a person. Episcopalians chant them out. Methodists sing them out. Congregationalists reason them out. Pentecostals shout them out. Baptists drown them out and Presbyterians freeze them out. Just remember this —whenever any church begins to think it is the only church then it has deteriorated to the point where it has ceased to be a church."

When Billy was speaking at a shipyard during the lunch hour, a man at a machine put down his tools midway of the talk and said, "Well, there'll be no more of that." He later confessed that he had been stealing materials from the firm and making things for his own benefit, while the others ate their noon meals.

*   *   *

A drunk man had to be led from the services at Kelvin one night. Two crusade officials took him home and witnessed to him, saying that Christ could give him a new life and victory over the drink habit.

Unknown to the crusade officials, the man's daughter was in a nearby bed and heard every word they said. The next night she went to the services at Kelvin and accepted Christ.

She went back home and began to live like a Christian. The father noted such a radiant change in his daughter that he returned to Kelvin and made the same decision when the invitation was given.

Will It Last?

SCOFFS AT EVANGELIST BILLY GRAHAM'S CRUSADE ARE BEING drowned in a sea of incredible statistics.

But as the skeptics go down for the last time they gurgle one final question, "Will it last?"

A Glasgow mother gave a partial answer to the question

in a letter to Billy. "I give thanks to God for sending you to us," she wrote. She told how her son, a thirteen-year-old, had gone forward at one of Billy's meetings and had never gone back on the decision which brought such "peace and happiness" to their home. The decision referred to by the mother was not made during the All-Scotland Crusade. It was made at a church service in 1947 when Billy, an unknown evangelist, held a series of meetings in Glasgow. Added the mother, "He has served for nearly two years in Her Majesty's forces and he is still taking every opportunity to witness for his Lord."

Billy readily admits that not all of the decisions will last. "The Bible clearly teaches," he says, "that not all of the decisions during the days of Christ lasted. Some of the seed fell on rocky ground and was blown away. Some of it fell on poor soil and failed to take root. But other seed fell on good earth and grew."

For the critics who want an answer they can reach out and touch, Billy usually gives his own testimony. He knows that people can argue with the Bible and disagree with the church, but is aware of the fact that so far the world hasn't come up with an answer to a transformed life.

He says, "Twenty years ago as a boy of sixteen, I walked forward and made a decision at an evangelistic meeting like this. My mother had talked me into attending by saying that a fighting preacher, Mordecai Ham, was holding the services. I figured if there was going to be a fight down at the church I wanted to see it. I didn't make a decision the first night. The preacher made me mad. Said I was a sinner. But I went back the next night and the next. Soon I realized that I had broken God's law. I had broken the Ten Commandments and I hadn't lived up to the Sermon on the Mount. I had come far short of the glory of God, which is Jesus Christ.

"I accepted by faith the words of the Bible that Christ

loved me enough to die for me. I made a calm, quiet resolve in my heart to live for Him from that moment on. That was twenty years ago. I have lasted. Cliff Barrows has lasted. Colleen Townsend, a former movie starlet, has lasted. I know hundreds of factory workers, business executives, and professional people who have lasted.

"We're not strong enough to hold onto Christ. He holds onto us. There is a doctor in Michigan who was on the alcoholic skids until about three years ago. His practice was gone and his family had about given up hope for him when he was converted in a campaign. After the decision he did an aboutface. His practice is now booming and he has a happy Christian home.

"An acquaintance cornered the doctor recently and said, 'Now tell me the truth, Doc, if you were all alone where there was no possibility of anyone ever finding out, wouldn't you take another drink? Let's be honest with each other.' The doctor thought for a minute before replying, 'Yes, if I were all alone I think I would take another drink.' After a short pause he added, 'But I'm never alone. Christ is with me.'"

Unlike many evangelists of the past who left converts to flounder for themselves after a campaign was over, Billy has a follow-up organization which keeps in touch for at least six months with each person making a decision. Men, women, and children are provided materials and encouraged to read the Bible, pray regularly, witness for Christ, and get active in a church.

When a decision is made at the services, the person writes down the church of his choice. The church is notified immediately, with a request that the convert be contacted at once. But Billy goes one step further. He checks up on the preacher. If the pastor rests on his dignity too long, Billy sends the convert's name to another church.

During the Harringay crusade in London, the Archbishop of Canterbury was visiting one afternoon with a parish minister. The minister had received two cards with the names of people who had made decisions. "You had better call on those people at once," the Archbishop warned. "If you don't, Billy Graham will send their names to a Baptist church."

*　　*　　*

Jack House, a popular reporter for The Glasgow *Evening News*, began his report on a Billy Graham meeting:

"Blessed is he that expecteth nothing, for he shall not be disappointed."

In his story he criticized Song Leader Cliff Barrows, described the "gravelly voice" of Soloist George Beverly Shea, and said Billy Graham "did not impress me in the least."

He concluded:

"May I say quite frankly, that after an evening as boring as any I've ever had in any hall, the final scene (when converts came) nauseated me."

Billy Graham made no reply, but residents of Glasgow bombarded the office of The *Evening News* with stinging protests. They had been told how Billy came to Scotland at the request of ministers and that he and team members were paying their own way.

Some of the letter comments:

"This was not the way Jack built the House we know" . . . "It is abundantly clear that Jack House knows nothing of the power of the gospel of Jesus Christ" . . . "Would that his pen were employed for God instead of the devil" . . . "Jack House has always been in my estimation a great journalist, and it is a pity he expected more than finding 'God' through 'Jesus Christ' in Kelvin Hall" . . . "As one of your constant readers may I say how ashamed I am that an obviously Christian man like Billy Graham should be so scurrilously treated in your paper."

Two People Talk

THE HOTEL CHAMBERMAID WALKED INTO MY ROOM TO CHECK its condition just as I was preparing to leave for the services.

She appeared to be a shriveled little woman of about fifty and, unlike most Scots, she rarely smiled. It was evident that life held few pleasures for her.

For a number of days, in cleaning the room, she had noticed all the clippings around my typewriter about Billy Graham, and assumed that I was a member of his team.

Just to make conversation, she asked: "Well, how is the campaign going?"

"Wonderful," I replied.

She frowned and straightened up the bed before replying:

"Sometimes I doubt whether there really is a God. And if there is, He can't be a very just God. I don't see why He makes my life so hard. My health has never been good, but I have to put in long hours while others seem to prosper without working too much. It just doesn't seem right.

"And I know that God doesn't answer prayers. Before my mother and father died, I prayed as hard as I could that God would spare them, but He didn't. All three of my brothers died in the last few years. I prayed for them, too, but it didn't do any good."

Praying silently under my breath for wisdom and words to help this unhappy woman, I said: "You know, the Bible teaches that before we can pray for others there is something we must do, with a sincere heart. We must pray, 'God have mercy on me, a sinner,' and then accept by faith that Jesus Christ, the Son of God, is 'the way, the truth, and the life.' "

That didn't make sense to her, and she continued grumbling, painting God as an ethereal grouch. Nothing I said seemed to have any effect.

Then, just as she was preparing to leave the room, a different approach seemed to come, and I said:

"You told me about some of your troubles. I'd like to tell you some of mine if you will listen a minute. I'm a newspaperman, not a preacher.

"Things are going well for me now, but it hasn't always been like that. Four years ago I was on the verge of bankruptcy. My family had already left me once and it looked as if my wife and children would have to leave again. I was just no good, and knew it. I was what the world regards as a hopeless alcoholic—had already lost one good job because of drinking and was about to lose another. Everything I did seemed to be wrong.

"I prayed every kind of prayer that I knew how to pray, but it was just like talking to a blank wall. Nothing worked."

For the first time, the woman showed interest, and asked to hear more. She stood quietly and listened:

"I drank socially for several years, and never had much trouble with the stuff, but during World War II, when I was publishing a Navy newspaper in Brazil, I crossed the narrow borderline that divides the social drinker from the alcoholic.

"After the war I left my home town (LaGrange, Ga.) and took my family to Chattanooga, Tenn., where I got a job as night editor of the Associated Press.

"After three years the Associated Press fired me. I deserved to be fired. Soon afterwards I got a job with Chattanooga's afternoon daily, *The News-Free Press*. I don't know why they gave me a job, because I didn't deserve one. To show my appreciation, I tried to stop drinking, but I couldn't.

"One day I was sitting in the office and noticed a little squib in the paper that said a man by the name of Dr. Fred Garland was going to tell his life story at a church in Chattanooga that night. The clipping indicated he had lived quite a life and I asked the city editor about going out to write a human interest piece. He said okay. I didn't have any interest in Fred Garland. I didn't have any interest in the church, or the Jesus Christ he was going to talk about. The only reason I wanted to do the story was the time and half-time I would get for working at night.

"I sat on the front row with a photographer and heard an incredible story—about a 'boy wonder' in show business, who let drink, dope, and crime reduce him to the point where he walked barefooted along the same streets on which he had once seen his name in lights. And he told of how his life had been transformed as he hung on the bars of Tombs Prison in New York City, called out to God and asked for mercy.

"He gave an invitation that night for people in the church to come forward and begin a new life in Christ. I knew that I should go, but didn't. I was afraid of what the photographer would think. I found out later he had been praying for me.

"Dr. Garland dismissed the congregation and came over to where I was standing. He said, 'I appreciate the publicity you are going to give me, but there's something more important. I want to ask you a question. Wouldn't you like to commit your life to Christ?' My reply was, 'I don't understand too much what it's all about, but if He can do for me what He has done for you, I would like to. I can look into your face and tell you're a happy man. I'm miserable.'

"He asked me to go into a little side room with him, where he asked if I would kneel with him in prayer. I had never knelt sincerely and prayed.

"Dr. Garland opened the Bible and showed me with Scripture that sin was my trouble, not alcohol. After the life I had lived, it didn't take much to convince me I was a sinner.

"Then he told me the simple story of Jesus, in a way that had never made sense to me before—how the Son of God came down from His home in heaven and loved a miserable, wretched, no good individual like George Burnham enough to die for him. The story broke my heart. He showed me a verse which said, 'If any man be in Christ, he is a new creature: old things are passed away; behold, all things are become new.'

" 'George,' he said, 'you can wipe out the past and become a new creature in Christ if you will, by faith, surrender your life to Him, right now. You don't have to understand all about it. Just let go and let God. He will transform your life.'

"That night, by faith, I surrendered my life to Christ and a strange, wonderful peace came into my heart as I knelt there on the floor. I felt different, somehow, when I got to my feet.

"We have a happy, Christian home now. Each day, with my wife and children, we read the Word of God and then kneel as a family to thank Him for all that we have. We wouldn't have a home if Jesus hadn't been invited in—to be our guest, advisor, and friend."

The little cleaning woman had dropped her head, but her eyes came up when I said:

"You lost both your father and mother. So did I, within six months of each other. But, you know, it's different when a person dies in Christ. My mother and father, bless their hearts, died without one worry. They knew where they were going and they knew that every child would be with them again soon.

"But such assurance isn't all that Christ gives to us. I read in the Bible one night where He will pick us up out of the dust of the earth and let us associate with princes, even the princes of our people. The first time I read that was one midnight in the Mayflower Hotel at Washington, D. C. The next morning I had breakfast with the President of the United States. Last year I had a talk with the Archbishop of Canterbury, the man who placed the crown on the head of the Queen of England. I had interviews with some of the leading political and military figures of Great Britain and Europe, and I have probably written more personal stories about Billy Graham than any living man.

"Please don't think that I'm boasting about my ability. God gets the credit. I was a hopeless alcoholic, on a greased slide to oblivion and, just like He promised, He picked me up out of the dust of the earth and let me associate with princes.

"He can do the same for you."

The shriveled little woman swallowed before speaking:

"I had never heard it quite like that before. I'm going to my room for a while. Maybe God will help me with my life."

And she turned and left the room!

(The final outcome of the chambermaid's case was never discovered, because of a 120,000,000 to one chance.

(Someone from among the millions in the United States picked up a newspaper one day, read the story from Scotland, and sent the paper to the unidentified chambermaid at an unnamed hotel in Glasgow.

(She read the story and knew immediately that she was the subject. It made her angry. She didn't object to the facts in the story, with one exception.

("Mr. Burnham," she said, "you referred to me as a woman of about fifty. For your information, I am thirty-four years old!"

(It looked as if I had committed the unpardonable sin, wounding the vanity of a woman, but I apologized every day for the next two weeks. The chambermaid and I were friends again when the campaign ended. She said it was her intention to spend much time in prayer, seeking peace with God.)

Scottish Thrift

THE WORLD, IT SEEMS, HAS MISTAKEN INTELLIGENT THRIFT IN Scotland for penny-pinching. Thousands of jokes have been told with laughter at the expense of the miserly Scot. But the joke appears to be on the jokers.

At the risk of being charged with losing all my reportorial marbles, I must state that Scots are generous people. They're not extravagant or wasteful, but do a better job of grappling for the after-dinner check than many Americans. The practice of tying shoes and waving at friends just as the check arrives has been developed to a fine art by thousands of the so-called smart set in the United States.

Collections at the crusade, which go to the local committee and not Billy Graham, were above the U. S. average, with close to $2,000 given each night.

An aged woman wrote that she watched the Kelvin meeting on television and was enclosing 100 pounds ($280), so that the work of Jesus Christ might spread throughout Scotland. Youngsters in a children's home collected their pennies and shillings to make an investment in religion instead of candy. A man wrote from Aberdeen saying that he wished to make a sizable contribution and said, "I trust that the fund has not been closed." In another letter, a nine-year-old girl enclosed ten shillings ($1.40) she had saved and said that in addition to giving her money she had given her life to Jesus Christ.

In sharp contrast to several European countries, where money flows like water and morality has deteriorated like a rotten apple, the people of Scotland are not tip-happy. Some Scots who deal with the public will accept a tip with sincere thanks, but if it is too much they will decline part of the money. Others will not accept anything.

* * *

Bev Shea, soloist for the Billy Graham team, was riding with his family and a friend in the busy streets of Edinburgh and came to a crowded intersection where a smartly uniformed bobbie was directing traffic. Unsure of the route to his destination, he asked directions of the policeman. Leaving his traffic duties, the officer came over to the car but had to admit that he didn't know the location in question. He asked the name of the people to be visited and said, "Wait a minute." To Bev's surprise the policeman walked about fifty yards away to a telephone booth and obtained the information desired. Draw your own contrasts.

* * *

Just a few years ago Louis Evans Jr. and Colleen Townsend were popular favorites among the young set in Hollywood. Evans' father was a famous preacher and Colleen was a budding movie starlet. They had everything, seemingly, that life had to offer. Now married and the parents of two beautiful children, they are living in a plainly furnished basement in Edinburgh, where Louis is studying for the ministry. The basement had accumulated years of filth before they moved in and cleaned it up. After the days of study are over they are going to the mission field where they will devote themselves to cleaning up many more of life's basements.

*   *   *

Crusade Items:

An estimated 400 people gave up their tickets at each service and spent the time praying in an "upper room" of the hall. While Billy preached they prayed. . . . Almost as much mail came from America, denouncing the "nauseating" article by Jack House, as came from Scotland. . . . A picture filmed by Billy during the crusade will be in color and on wide screen, depicting much of Scotland's religious history. . . . Salaries of ministers in the Church of England are 550 pounds net annually ($1,540). Salaries for Methodists, Baptists, and Presbyterians are less. Many pastors have to take part-time jobs to pay monthly bills.

Solving a Problem

AN AMERICAN PREACHER, WHO MAY AS WELL GO UNNAMED, made a special trip to Great Britain before the start of Billy's Scotland Crusade.

He was not there to herald the coming of the American evangelist. He was there to speak against Billy Graham.

The preacher, who also publishes a magazine, went up and down the country, urging the people not to listen to the young upstart. He told them Billy had no real standing in his own country and that he preached a false gospel.

The reason for the special trip was that Billy would not denounce all except the fundamental faith. Billy doesn't denounce any faith. He preaches the positive message of Jesus Christ.

After his return to the United States, the preacher-editor continued to write torrid articles against Billy.

In a conversation one night, Billy said:

"You know, deep down in my heart, I was beginning to resent the man. He was trying to destroy my ministry. As far as I know he has never attended one of my meetings—wouldn't know him if I met him on the street.

"Resentment is a sin and I couldn't go on the platform at Kelvin Hall with resentment in my heart. I couldn't ask those people to repent and love their neighbors if I had sin in my own heart.

"One afternoon, all alone in my room at the hotel, I fell on my knees before God and prayed. I told God that I was going to stay on my knees until He instilled a genuine love in my heart for the man. And I stayed there, asking God to do what I could not do as a human. After a considerable time God answered my prayer and when I stood to my feet I had a genuine love for him.

"I sat down and wrote the man a letter, telling him of my resentment and of the victory that God had given. I told him that if he ever attended one of my meetings he would be greeted in Christian love."

The letter was mailed, but the resulting answer was in the same vein as other disparaging articles.

Billy's love remained. He had conquered his problem. The problem of the other man remains.

Church Revolution

THE REVOLUTION AGAINST MERE RITUAL HAS SPREAD AMONG the churches in Scotland. Spearheaded by the warm, old-fashioned services held by Billy Graham, the revolt against cold program procedure was carried forward by the ministers.

Scores of preachers in Scotland are giving invitations to come forward and confess Christ for the first time in their ministry. This is regarded by churchmen as the most significant phase of the All-Scotland Crusade.

It may be difficult for Americans to understand the impact of such a move because such invitations are common in many United States churches, but not so in Scotland, where tradition and ritual have dominated the austere services. After attending a service at Kelvin, the Rev. Bernard Hearfield, pastor of Lamlock Presbyterian Church, decided to break away from his usual program and hold an evangelistic meeting. On the following Sunday he did so and twenty members of his congregation walked forward. "I have long felt such a thing was needed," he said. "The Billy Graham rallies have created the kind of climate of thought in which it could be done without provoking a riot."

Many other ministers also are asking for decisions at the end of their sermons. The Rev. John Hamilton, redhaired ex-marine, minister of Tollcross Park Church, did so one Sunday. Six people came forward. After the service he said, "This has been one of the greatest days I have known in my ministry. I claim no credit." In three weeks seventeen came forward at the Rev. George McNeill's Baptist Church.

Hundreds of invitations were given nightly by ministers of Scotland, England, Wales, and Ireland at relay points where people gathered to hear the services. A Church of Scotland minister gave an invitation in his church and was practically dumfounded when twenty-five people walked down the aisles. The next day he sought out the chairman of the crusade, the Rev. Tom Allan, told him what had happened and asked, "Now that I've got them, what am I going to do with them?" He was advised first of all to start a Bible class, second to begin a weekly prayer meeting, and then to begin a regular visitation program in the neighborhood with the new converts doing the visiting. The remarkable thing about this conversation was that the Rev. Allan, who was doing the advising, had given the first invitation in his own ministry a few nights previously. The ministers of Scotland have caught a vision and are helping each other.

This has been one of the paramount prayers of the American evangelistic team—that the ministers and church people of Scotland will focus their eyes on Christ instead of Billy Graham.

*   *   *

Chain Reaction:

Associate Evangelist Howard Butt gave an invitation at a factory in a nearby town. A number of hands were raised. Songleader Cliff Barrows noticed that the boss of the factory was among those making a decision. Others in the factory noted it in the next few days, too, when the boss put into action his new beliefs. He worked and witnessed for Christ.

It led to more decisions. A father went to the boss and said, "My fourteen-year-old son attended one of the services at Kelvin and made a decision. I don't know what to do with him. My wife and I have never had much use for the church."

The boss suggested that the father let him get two tickets for Kelvin so he could see for himself what his boy had seen. The father said he didn't think it would do any good but consented to give it a try.

Together with his wife, he went to the hall. During the service they were convicted of their own sinful lives and walked forward when the invitation was given.

The entire family is now living for Christ. They are witnessing along with the boss about the change in their lives. And the chain is still unwinding.

* * *

"I have received word that practically every church in Nashville, Tenn., held prayer meetings for Glasgow," Billy Graham told 17,000 Scots from the pulpit.

He added, "You would have to be from the Southern part of the United States to appreciate this, but an Episcopal rector led the prayer meeting at Nashville's First Baptist Church. Brother, that's revival."

The evangelist also had a report that 400 people in Barcelona, Spain, were on their knees every morning from 6:30 to 7:30 praying for Glasgow.

The head of a tribe in Northern India, headhunters only forty years ago, wrote Billy to say that an average of 400 tribesmen pray every day for Glasgow.

Children at a school in Mexico wrote Billy they would pray for him daily.

A full-blooded Indian from Montana wrote: "The people of the Sioux Reservation are praying for you and for the city of Glasgow."

* * *

Crusade Items:

"Against all doubts and sneers can be placed the undeniable fact that both inside Kelvin Hall and outside, Dr.

Graham has stirred up spiritual thought in a way that did not seem possible before he came. He has made religion news again; he has reminded professing Christians everywhere of obligations they had conveniently forgotten; he has bequeathed to our native clergy a legacy of renewed interest in God's Word, a legacy for them to exploit when he has gone."—Glasgow *Evening Citizen.*

"Don't let anyone tell you Christianity is for old ladies and sissies. It takes steel in your backbone. It takes courage to commit yourself to Jesus Christ."—Howard Butt.

"I don't know whether Billy Graham realizes what he has started in England with the meetings at Harringay. At a meeting recently, hundreds of churches in England and Wales pledged themselves to evangelize the nation for God this year."—Dr. F. Copland-Simmons, moderator of Free Church, Federal Council, of England and Wales.

"I have never in my life seen it so easy to discuss religion, the church, the Bible, Christianity, and things pertaining to the Kingdom of God."—Minister from Dunoon in conversation with Associate Evangelist Grady Wilson.

Rumors Spread

RUMORS WERE SPREAD IN THE UNITED STATES DURING THE Scotland meeting that Billy Graham had compromised his hard-hitting old-fashioned sermons from the Bible in favor of a modern social gospel more pleasing to man. The reports were not true. He told people of Scotland what the Bible has to say and let the chips fall.

Billy preached the same gospel that he preached in New York, New Orleans, Nashville, Detroit, Chattanooga, Los Angeles, and Portland.

The heart of his message, then and now, is that all are sinners—the wages of sin is eternal separation from God—the blood of Jesus Christ is the only cure for sin—and man will never get to heaven unless he repents and surrenders his will to do the will of God.

He preaches the Bible from Genesis to Revelation as the Word of God. Another interpretation, which has been labeled modernism, says that the Bible contains the Word of God but that many of its stories are myths and fairy tales.

In an address at Kelvin, Billy said, "There is no such thing as a social gospel. The gospel is the good news that Jesus Christ died to save sinners. It has social implications, however, of man's relations to man, but the gospel is the good news."

The reports were spread by a small core of ministers and Christian workers who want Billy to deviate from his main objective—winning people for Christ, and denounce various groups for their contrary sideline beliefs. Billy lets the Bible do all his denouncing. He has one message: "Jesus Christ and Him crucified."

Dr. John R. Rice of Wheaton, Ill., often referred to as the dean of American evangelism, strongly endorsed the ministry of Billy during a visit to Scotland. After hearing several of the sermons at Kelvin he said, "Thank God for Billy Graham and members of his team. He is preaching the gospel of Jesus Christ in all its simplicity, authority, and power—like Dwight L. Moody and Billy Sunday. He preaches a plain message leading to a definite point—repentance and faith in Christ."

Dr. Rice, sixty-year-old Baptist and editor of *The Sword of The Lord*, likened Billy and his critics to a football game. "Have you ever noticed," he said, "that when a man runs fifteen yards in a game, he always seems to have plenty of interference, but when he gets loose on a long touchdown run, he has to get way out ahead of the interference and some of the blockers don't like to be left behind. What a wonderful sight it was to see those hundreds of people coming to Christ every night at Kelvin. I have been trying to tell people for years that God was not through and was going to do big things again.

"I followed the converts into the counseling room. Billy didn't tell them what church to join, but he told them to get into a good church where the Bible was preached."

Similar endorsements of Billy's ministry were made by several other visitors to Scotland: Dr. John Sutherland Bonnell; Dr. Louis Evans of Hollywood, Calif., and Dr. Rupert McGregor, president of the Montreat Association in North Carolina.

Practically all denominations in Great Britain placed their stamp of approval on the evangelist's work. Billy is a Baptist minister, but he never mentions denominations from the pulpit unless he is introducing a visitor. He stands there on the platform with a Bible in his hand and tells people what God has to say. It's as simple and profound as that.

*   *   *

Crusade Items:

Amidst all the hubbub of work in the crusade office, there was time for romance. Bob French, only bachelor on the Graham team, announced his engagement to Joyce Telfer, twenty-two, volunteer worker and daughter of a Glasgow minister. Bob, thirty, was a fighter pilot during the war. He was shot down over Germany and was a prisoner for sixteen months. . . . During his brief stay in Scotland, Dr. John R. Rice led a taxi driver and Chicago reporter to confess Christ as Lord and Saviour. . . . There is to be no more Sunday golf on Edinburgh's municipal courses. Before the vote was taken by officials, Bailie J. G. Dunbar said: "There is no use in Billy Graham coming to Edinburgh if the corporation accepts a proposal which cuts across all he is trying to do." Added Councillor Allan Scott: "We are the capital city of Scotland and as a God-loving and fearing people we must take a stand, and our thoughts must be with the church."

*   *   *

Crusade Quotes:

"I believe with all my soul that it is possible for a man to serve God in the way he conducts his affairs every day, that it is possible for a man to live with Jesus Christ in the traffic of everyday activity."—Howard Butt.

"The Lord answers my prayers everywhere but on the golf course."—Billy Graham, who shoots cross-handed and usually records a score ranging from eighty-five to 105.

Relay in Belfast

THE GAY CITY OF BELFAST, WHERE SMILING IRISHMEN PUT their best into a zest for living, saw something on a Saturday night that probably will never be duplicated by any city in America.

Over 4,000 citizens, most of them young people, overflowed in two big assembly halls to hear a preacher. This is unusual enough in itself on Saturday night, but the preacher was not in Belfast. He was in Glasgow, Scotland.

The restless Irish, who like to sing or dance a jig at the drop of a plumed hat, sat quietly in the two halls for over an hour and a half as they listened to a loudspeaker relaying the Billy Graham evangelistic service from Glasgow, 200 miles away.

An estimated 1,000,000 people in about 700 halls throughout Great Britain were doing the same thing. In one community a woman who lived across the street from the hall was stubborn about giving up her telephone line, but finally yielded.

It's just possible that many bored Americans rushing madly about trying to get entertained may not be able to visualize such a relay service. Neither could I. So I took a night boat to Belfast for a first-hand look. The two halls filled early, and in the Wellington assembly there were people sitting in the aisles some fifteen minutes before Cliff Barrows began leading his 1,500 voice choir in the crusade theme song, "Blessed Assurance." When Cliff asked all those in Glasgow's Kelvin Hall to wave their songbooks, the people in Ireland waved theirs too. He then led the congregation in singing Scotland's favorite, "The Twenty-third Psalm" to the tune of "Crimond." A choir leader with headphones led the Irish congregation in singing the same song.

The great throng listened quietly as Dr. Paul Rees of Minneapolis read from the Bible and Dr. Nevile Davidson prayed. People of Ireland sat with rapt expressions as the great voice of Bev Shea boomed over the loudspeaker, "Sing Me a Song of Sharon's Rose."

After this, Cliff got a little fancy, but he may never know just how fancy, on the song, "Revive Us Again." He had it set up that the people in Kelvin Hall would sing "Hallelujah," then remain quiet while the people in an adjoining hall sang, "Thine the Glory." What he didn't know was that "Hallelujah" was sung in Scotland, and "Thine the Glory" in Ireland. This should go down in history as the greatest international choir ever assembled. When the collection was taken in Scotland, it was also taken in Ireland to pay for line tolls.

Billy Graham stepped onto the platform and faced three different mediums: 17,000 in Kelvin, several thousand by closed circuit TV in the adjoining hall, and about 1,000,-000 at relay points. After warming to his difficult task he lashed out at the world's indifference to the gospel of Jesus Christ. "People today have plenty of time," he said, "to read the newspapers and watch TV, but they just don't have time to read the Bible. I solemnly warn those people that they are heading for destruction and hell."

Shooting verses from the Bible in machine-gun fashion, he cautioned members of churches against mistaking an intellectual belief in Christ for a heart surrender. "You can join every church in the world," Billy said, "but it won't get you to heaven. The Bible teaches there has to come a moment in your life when you surrender your will to Christ. Have you done that?" There was a moment's pause in Scotland. You could have heard a pin drop in Ireland. A ministerial student listening to a relay service at the University of Edinburgh was serving as counselor at a relay meeting. Billy asked over the loudspeaker if the people knew Christ or just knew about Him. The student snatched off his counselor badge and threw it onto the floor before marching forward. He said, "I entered the ministry as a career. Now I want to receive Christ into my heart."

At the finish of his message in Kelvin, Billy asked the people who wanted to receive Christ to come forward. He asked those watching on TV and those listening to the relay to do the same thing. Several hundred moved forward at

Kelvin, about thirty walked to the front in Belfast, an estimated 1,500 went to the front of halls throughout Great Britain.

In the face of all this, some cynics continue to insist that the people are moved by hypnotism or emotionalism instead of God. A leading writer in Britain said, "It is something in the eyes of Billy Graham that does it." Maybe so, but Billy hasn't been in Ireland since 1947.

A Million Dollars

BILLY DID NOT REFER TO ACTRESS SUSAN HAYWARD BY NAME, but remarked during a Kelvin address:

"I read in a newspaper report that one of our most beautiful Hollywood stars—thirty-five years of age, a million dollars in the bank, name known all over the world, an Academy Award winner—has been taken to a hospital suffering from an overdose of sleeping pills.

"I have been in Hollywood many times. Many of the people are the most miserable you've ever met. They find that all the glamor does not satisfy the soul. Happiness is only found in Christ."

❄   ❄   ❄

Billy made one of his brief answers to criticism in Glasgow. Some of the watchdog citizens who cried "emotionalism," "hypnotism," and even urged him to hold special services for animals, noticed that occasionally a child would be crying as he walked forward to make a decision for Christ. Criticism was hot.

To this the evangelist replied, "It's a funny thing children can go to the pictures and see gangsters shooting it out in grim battle, cowboys in hair-raising situations, and the most moving love scenes which upset them emotionally. But if they shed one tear for God it's a terrible thing. Something is wrong in the thinking of a world where this situation exists."

*   *   *

Song Director Cliff Barrows highly praised the engineering accomplishments that made it possible for a choir in Bangor, Wales, to sing for the Scots at Glasgow's Kelvin Hall. When the song came over the loudspeaker, he said, "I think there must be some angels who are joining in along the line." He remarked, "We heard the song of the Lord in a very literal sense—the song from voices in Wales and Glasgow—but prior to the song was the work of others whose engineering labors made the song possible. It's a simple thing to say, but it is very true that if we work for Him today we will sing for Him tomorrow."

*   *   *

A debate was held by the Glasgow University Union and the Oxford Union Society on the motion: "That Billy Graham is an Undesirable Immigrant." While the debate was in progress, Billy was addressing about 80,000 people of Scotland at Ibrox Stadium.

Anxious Policeman

A BURLY POLICEMAN GRABBED ASSOCIATE EVANGELIST Howard Butt by the arm as the young Texan and Billy Graham threaded their way through a crowd of 25,000 for the final service at Glasgow's Kelvin Hall.

"Mr. Butt," said the officer, "I can't attend the service tonight because I'm on duty, but I want to accept Christ. Will you help me?"

As thousands streamed past, Howard took the policeman by the hand and carefully told him the simple steps in a surrender to Christ. With bowed heads they prayed, and then thanked God. Before hurrying off to duty the beaming officer said, "I'm going to take my stand publicly tomorrow."

Some 6,000 had to stand outside in drizzling rain for the last service, with 19,000 jammed inside. Before the start of the main service Billy went outside, gave a brief message and invitation. Over 125 responded. After returning to the main platform he said, "This is God's doing. Give Him all the praise, honor, and glory. I hope the name Billy Graham soon disappears from your lips. I am here as a messenger of Jesus Christ and I pray that the people of Scotland will talk about Him."

Said the Rev. Tom Allan, "For thousands, Kelvin has proved to be the very gates of heaven. This hall may prove to be the turning point in the religious history of Scotland." Added Billy, "This will not be the last time we visit Scotland." The words brought a thunderous burst of applause.

Crusade Items:

Some Glasgow school teachers said Billy violated their wishes when he spoke to 10,000 children and asked for a show of hands from those who would like to accept Christ. He didn't ask them to come forward. Billy replied that he had not been asked to skip the invitation. Children had to have written permission from parents. . . . "Daddy, why don't these people speak good English so that we can understand them?" asked nine-year-old Virginia Graham. . . . "There is no such thing as success outside of Jesus Christ." Billy Graham.

Communist Reaction

THE TRUE WORTH OF BILLY'S CRUSADE CAN BE GAUGED BY THE vast amount of smear space devoted to him by Glasgow's Communist publication, *The Word.*

One issue gave practically all of its first three pages to blasts against Billy, a spotlight indication that the Communists regard his simple message as one of the greatest dangers they face. Here are a few samples of Red reporting, under the headline "Glasgow, Prey for Billy Graham":

"Billy Graham has been allowed by the Presbytery of Glasglow to register the church of God as a den of thieves. I congratulate the Presbytery. Reaction precedes revolution. Billy Graham and his agents, unless repudiated by the Presbytery, will destroy the church." (The Communists, it seems, never bother about making sense. In attacking Billy, they defend the church they hate.)

"After six weeks Billy will go back to London for further revival activity and Glasgow will return to its humdrum church apathy. In due course Billy will return to the states conscious of his greatness. He will have lived well. He will have been the subject of many prayers. He will have traveled much. And he will have left precisely no effect on the world." (This party line bears a vaguely familiar resemblance to many critics of the evangelist in America.)

"The miracles of folly will never cease until the workers go into action and say with Jesus that the temple has become a den of thieves, a very beautiful den, a lavishly furnished den, but still a den with lies, corruption, and smooth talk broadcast throughout the country." (The Reds know Scripture. They use it to fight preachers instead of help people.)

In commenting on the fact that Billy draws a salary of $15,000 a year and is building a new house to give his family more living space, the article says, "What intolerable hypocrisy and falsehood when one considers how the poor live in the U.S. and in Glasgow. The explanation about the extra house is nonsense unless the man wants such houseroom for all families. But he does not say so and obviously does not think so, in which case he does not preach the gospel of the Son of Man. He is therefore no missionary of Jesus. And the study. Did Jesus, who had nowhere to lay His head, have a study? And what need has an ignoramus like Billy Graham of a study?"

(Billy's salary, paid by the trust funds he heads at Minneapolis, is less than that drawn by many preachers in the United States. Free-will offerings supply the fund. He accepts no love offerings. The house he now lives in at Montreat, N. C., with a wife and four children has two bedrooms. He is not building an extra house. He will sell the old in order to get the new, which will be larger but not elaborate. Any American with four children will understand why he needs a study.)

"There is a lot of explanation given as to how Billy Graham spends his income. We are assured that not a penny comes from the churches, ministers, or countries that invite him to run campaigns. If this is true, then his activity is subsidized by the American Wall Street interests. It is one way or the other. The whole point is that he lives well, spreading what is really a definite anti-Christian and pro-capitalist gospel in the name of Jesus Christ, as he prefers to state."

(Billy is one of the world's softest touches. From his salary he gives away hundreds of dollars each year to destitute churches and to aid missionaries. His friends have formed a little conspiracy to keep him from giving away everything he owns. In Glasgow he gave away his golf clubs three times in one week to friends, not in exasperation for poor play but because they needed clubs. The friends thanked him for the clubs but accidently forgot to take them. Admire one of his ties and he'll probably take it off and give it to you.)

"Obviously it is worldly happiness and easy living to be an evangelist. And what good does it do? Precisely no good at all. No one is benefited except the evangelist."

(Thousands of people in America and Scotland will look you straight in the eye and tell you that their lives have been miraculously changed after listening to the gospel of Jesus Christ as proclaimed by Billy Graham and other preachers.)

After his Berlin meeting the previous year, the Communist paper in Germany gave a lurid account of Billy taking his team to a night club, buying liquor by the case, and then getting thrown in jail for trying to slip out without paying the bill. The Reds could not be content with just an ordinary little lie. It had to be a whopper, and was so ridiculous that it defeated their objective.

Clear and Simple

BILLY GRAHAM, IN A NOON TALK TO PREACHERS, CLIMAXED the crusade with the plainest message of his phenomenal ministry.

And when he had finished, over 1,000 clergymen of Scotland made decisions to rededicate their lives to God. These same men had objected to such an invitation for the people at the start of the campaign.

Ministers overflowed the Renfield Street Church. During his address, Billy summarized the crusade—"What has happened, why did it happen and what lies ahead?" But near the end he stated:

"I may be completely out of order in doing this, but I have some suggestions for you ministers. When you go into the pulpit next Sunday, preach with clarity and simplicity. Preach to the people in language they can understand. The fact that you shoot over the heads of your congregation doesn't prove you have superior ammunition. It just proves you can't shoot.

"And preach with your natural voices. If many of you went into a grocery store and ordered a loaf of bread in the sing-song manner you affect in the pulpit, you would never get the bread because the clerk wouldn't be able to understand you. You don't talk in a chant. Then why preach that way? The reason theaters are filled and churches are empty is that the people can understand what is being said in a theater.

"I would like to also stress the importance of making sure that you have a gospel to preach. The pastor of a leading Glasgow church came to me the other day and said, 'Billy, I don't have a gospel for my people.' People don't want good advice. They want the good news of Jesus Christ —'For God so loved the world, that he gave his only begotten Son, that whosoever believeth in him should not perish, but have everlasting life.' Preach the Bible with authority.

"Early in my ministry I was doing a lot of preaching but didn't have any power. One day I fell on my knees and said, 'Oh, God, I am going to have to get out of the ministry unless I find a message with power.' As I prayed I accepted by faith the Bible as the inspired Word of God. From that moment my ministry has been different."

Billy urged the ministers to preach the Bible with urgency and give the people an opportunity to accept Christ. "Go into your pulpits," he said, "and preach a gospel message. Then ask for decisions and rededications."

Scotland before the crusade had practically abandoned such an invitation. Ministers said it was obsolete, but thousands changed their minds and methods.

In discussing what happened in Scotland during the six-weeks' crusade, Billy stated, "People are no longer indifferent about religion, and the greatest problem facing the clergy is indifference. Religion is the main topic of conversation in Scotland again. Newspaper reporters who made decisions during the campaign are forming a fellowship for study. A man told some of his friends in a club about two weeks ago that his wife had made a decision at Kelvin and that he noticed a difference in her. The man later went back to the club and told the same group he had accepted Christ.

"Revivals have broken out in small towns far from here as people listen to a voice over the relay. Churches are working together. A Baptist minister told me the other day he had never had much use for Presbyterians but had learned during the crusade to respect their work. Brother, that's revival. Maybe we can't agree on everything, but we can love one another.

"Thousands have accepted Christ and vows have been renewed. Paul Mickelson was sitting at his organ in an empty Kelvin Hall one afternoon when a workman walked up and said, 'I was an alcoholic and my home was wrecked, but since my conversion God has taken the desire for alcohol away from me and my home has been restored.' I saw a giant Highlander wearing kilts walk forward one night. He lived in some remote area north of here and told us later, 'All my life I've wanted God but didn't know where to find Him. Someone told me that people were finding Him here and I came down.'

"A social impact has been made on Scotland. A department store head said employes had come to him admitting thefts. Barlinnie Prison, which usually had fifty or sixty at religious services now has an average of 500. A businessman has instituted new relations with his workers.

"Churches have received a new breath of life. Ministers are taking old truths and feeding hungry people. One pastor told me his congregation had doubled.

"Now you ask why all this has happened. It has happened because people are hungry to hear the Word of God. It has happened in answer to the prayers of Christian people. As I have told you before, Glasgow, because of modern communications, is the most prayed-for city in the history of the Christian church. There were thousands of prayer meetings around the world. Four hundred lepers in Africa prayed for an hour every morning.

"It has happened because of the power of the Holy Spirit which convicted people of sin after the Word has been preached. It happened because there was a unity among the churches, because there was organization and publicity. Some have criticized the meetings, saying they cost too much. Let me tell you something. People don't mind spending money on all forms of pleasures and amusements, but when it comes to spending money to bring a man to Jesus Christ they yelp to high heavens. Such thinking is greed and God hates it."

Turning to the question of what lies ahead, Billy said: "If you ministers fail to go out and help these people who need spiritual growth, there could be a revolution of laymen in Scotland with the blessings outside rather than inside the church. There could well be a disaster unless the clergy takes its place of proper leadership.

"Our campaign has been like a short subject at a movie. The main feature is now about to go on. We have only scratched the surface. The main harvest is yet to come. As far as Billy Graham is concerned, I feel no glow of personal victory or triumph this morning. This has been God's doing and it is marvelous in our eyes."

Power of the Press

A MEETING, TUCKED OFF IN A SIDE ROOM OF A GLASGOW HALL, two weeks after the close of Scotland's greatest religious crusade, didn't draw a single headline. But a lot of headlines will develop from the meeting.

The session was called by editors and newspaper reporters for the purpose of officially organizing a Christian press fellowship. Representatives from practically every paper in Glasgow were present. All had either made first-time decisions for Christ or had re-dedicated their lives during the All-Scotland Crusade of Billy Graham. There seems little doubt that the effect on the lives of newspaper men and women will prove to be one of the most far-reaching results of Billy's campaign. Newspapers in Scotland have vast circulations, because of the compactness of the country.

Most of the reporters had gone to cover the crusade in Kelvin with an indifferent or cynical attitude. For some strange reason, the average reporter thinks that he is different from other people. But he isn't. He has the same hopes, fears, and problems as other people. As the reporters in Scotland listened, night after night, to the claims of the Bible, their attitudes changed. And they began to leave the press table and take their places with the hundreds of others standing at the front, seeking a new life of peace and assurance.

They stood up at the private press meeting in front of their fellow reporters and testified they had found it. It was my privilege to be invited as their first speaker. Sixteen men and one woman were present. Some had been told that it was impossible to be a Christian and a reporter at the same time. They hadn't been told that it was much harder to be a drunkard and a good reporter.

The group didn't need a speaker. One of their own members took his stand at the front. He spoke up boldly and told how he had wrecked his life and the life of his family while playing the role of a star reporter in a cocked hat. Afterwards he explained: "It was necessary for me to do that. There were men sitting in the room who knew about the life I had lived and I wanted to set them straight on what Christ had done for me."

The main thing that members of the group wanted to know was how they could be of intelligent service. With attitudes like that it is going to be a long time before they write "30" to the All-Scotland Crusade. Maybe the story will never end.

*   *   *

Items and Quotes:

Soloist George Beverly Shea had a new song recently—"I'm Forever Blowing Bubbles." His five-year-old son, Ronnie, put a piece of soap in a candy box and guess which piece papa bit into. . . . "The ingredients of war are found in the hearts of the world's inhabitants. Only a spiritual awakening can purge our hearts of the elements of war. In the last 3,000 years of history the world has known only 300 years of peace. Once in history a war was fought over a cow. It was the War of the Cow of Ciney and raged for three years, killing 20,000 men. Many of the wars have been fought for political and ideological reasons, but the Bible says, 'Come not they hence, even of your own lusts.' "—Billy Graham.

Two Handshakes

THE BISHOP OF BARKING, A GIANT OF A MAN WEARING KNEE britches, was the first person to greet Billy Graham when the American arrived for his first London campaign.

And the Bishop was the first to clasp his hand when

Billy came back to London after an incredibly successful crusade in Glasgow.

Circumstances surrounding the two meetings tell quite a story.

Because of the furor about the socialism incident mentioned previously, Billy was, on the first trip, probably the most unwelcome visitor to Britain since the Luftwaffe. He was denounced by the politicians and the press. Scores of ministers from the Church of England joined in the angry chorus.

It was at this point, when the ship landed, that the Bishop of Barking risked his future in the national church. He clasped Billy's hand and said: "If this campaign is a success, we'll give God all the credit. If it's a failure, I'll stand up in the boat with you and we'll go down together."

The campaign exceeded all expectations. Billy preached to an estimated 1,500,000, recorded over 40,000 decisions for Jesus Christ, and saw new life return to churches. The Archbishop of Canterbury was on the platform and 120,000 were inside Wembley for the closing service. London was followed by an even more successful tour of Europe.

Billy's second trip to London followed six weeks in Scotland. The Bishop of Barking, still wearing knee britches after phenomenal growth in clerical stature, walked forward as the train pulled into Euston Station. He gave the evangelist a warm, sincere welcome.

The press was there, but the hostility was gone. The church was solidly behind his Wembley meetings. "Next to the royal family, Billy is probably the best-known person in Britain today," the London *Daily Express* commented.

The newspaper continued:

"On Saturday afternoon Sir Anthony Eden's car, marked out by decorous election bills, will nose its way through the shopping crowds of Clapham and Battersea. The Prime

Minister of Britain will be traveling to meet the people. Three hours later Billy Graham will speak at Wembley. He will not travel to meet the people. The people of London will travel to meet him.

"A hundred thousand of them have already booked seats for that evening alone, more than may come to Sir Anthony throughout the whole (election) campaign. Sir Anthony, if re-elected, will bear our future in his hands. This election will mould great issues—peace, prosperity, war— yet if attendances at meetings are to be taken in evidence, the people are not greatly bothered. They are more interested in Dr. Graham. Should we condemn this preference? Of course not. Graham's own words about a religious revival will do more for peace than a Big Three meeting."

One year has made a lot of difference. I wonder if the Bishop of Barking has ever thought about all that has happened between the two occasions on which he shook the hand of Billy Graham.

Cold Bodies, Warm Hearts

A BITTER, BONE-CHILLING WIND SWEPT ACROSS THE HISTORIC turf at London's Wembley Stadium on a cloudy Saturday evening as 70,000 gathered to hear Billy Graham. Americans would not have gone to an open stadium on such a day to hear a preacher. But Americans are not as hungry or as disciplined as the people of England. Years of war and austerity have left their mark on the hardy people of this tiny island.

The beautiful stadium, where the sports champions of the world have performed, was immaculate down to the rolled red cinders of the speedway track. Signs pointed "To the Bars" and "To the Tote" for drinking and gambling, but these places were out of business for a night. A long red carpet was stretched all the way across the emerald turf from in front of the royal box to the speaker's platform. Two weeks earlier Queen Elizabeth sat in the box for the cup final soccer match. On this night, Mrs. Ruth Graham from Montreat, N. C., sat in the box with her ten-year-old daughter, Virginia.

A rustling went through the crowd as Billy stepped onto the carpet with the Bishop of Barking, who wore his familiar knee britches. Billy had a splitting headache. He had looked forward to the meeting with "fear and trembling, utterly dependent upon Almighty God."

A paralyzed woman with a radiant face, who had prayed long for this night, was lying flat on a push cart near the platform. Billy was almost past before he caught a glimpse of her amidst the crowd. He walked over and clasped her hand saying, "God bless you." She beamed.

Sitting in front-row seats were four "teddy boys" (zoot-suit hoodlums) from the heart of London's gangland. Dressed in long coats and drainpipe trousers, they nervously fingered their string ties. The leader, a powerfully built youth with razor scars on one side of his face said, "We heard this Graham bloke could put over the spiel. We wanted to see if he was just as good as on television."

Grady Wilson read the Eighth Psalm, with his voice bouncing all over the vast stadium, as technicians hurriedly tried to work the bugs out of the public address system. Words of welcome and praise were given by the Bishop of Barking and the Rev. F. D. Copland-Simmons. George Beverly Shea sang "Were You There When They Crucified My Lord?" Not a whisper could be heard from the 70,000 as America's most famous gospel singer breathed the stirring words. Music Director Cliff Barrows, who handles thousands of singers with effortless ease, led the throng in singing "The Lord's Prayer." The booming words could be heard for miles around.

A cold rain began to pepper down as the people sang. Umbrellas went up and raincoats went on. But few left. The rain stopped shortly after Billy went to the mike. Because of the frigid weather he wore a fawn raglan raincoat, a plain blue suit, and galoshes over his shoes.

He didn't leave the people in doubt for a moment about where he stood and what he would preach during the coming seven days at Wembley. "This is the work of God, not Billy Graham. I have come here again to preach the same message I preached at Harringay. I have come to give you the Bible warning that you must be born again or you will never see the Kingdom of Heaven. I have come to say that unless ye be converted ye shall likewise perish. I am determined to know nothing among you save Jesus Christ and Him crucified."

A Bible quotation in enormous letters covered the face of the race indicator at one end of the stadium. It said, "I am the way, the truth, and the life." Billy glanced at the quotation and said, "That is my text. Those are the words of Jesus. He didn't say, 'I am a way.' He said, 'I am the way. No man cometh unto the Father, but by me.'" He carefully explained the universality of sin, the consequences of sin, and the cure for sin—Jesus Christ. He said, "Jesus can lift every burden and enable you to walk out of Wembley Stadium a new person, but it takes more than a head knowledge. You must confess your sin and be willing to turn from it. You will never be able to understand how it happens, but it does. It happened to me. And it has happened to thousands of others. You accept Christ by faith. If you could understand it all, there would be no need for faith."

Billy asked the people to get up out of their seats, walk

quietly forward, and stand in front of the platform. A trickle started, but in moments a great stream was flowing forward. The surge continued until over 3,500 stood on Wembley's green turf.

The four teddy boys didn't go forward. They left their seats and walked quietly out of the stadium. There were no smart cracks. They were thinking.

Billy looked out over the people committing their lives to Christ and said, "All the scenes of Pentecost are being seen here again tonight." He had stated earlier, "This may not be what we have longed for. It may not be what some call revival. But I am convinced we are in the midst of a great spiritual awakening that is gathering momentum. This is the work of Almighty God."

The cold wind continued to sweep across Wembley Stadium, but it had lost its chilling effect for the thousands who stood with bowed heads and warm hearts.

A Fight Night

THE CHURCH HAS WAITED ALMOST 2,000 YEARS TO SEE THE things that happened in London.

When the Apostle Peter preached at Pentecost, the Bible says "about 3,000 souls" were added to the church. This figure was exceeded twice in consecutive services, under the worst possible conditions, by Billy Graham at Wembley.

But, the world being what it is, the momentous events

were shoved to the back pages by a fist fight between Rocky Marciano and Don Cockell, 6,000 miles away.

An estimated 50,000 people sat for two hours in a steady rainfall at Wembley on a Monday night to hear Billy preach an old-fashioned sermon on sin, repentance, and judgment. The rainfall became a downpour when the invitation was given for people to walk onto the turf and confess Christ before men as Lord and Saviour. Scores, then hundreds, then thousands came, forming a cross of people under a sea of umbrellas.

A total of 3,033 signed cards. At the first service on Saturday there were 3,500 decisions. "If this isn't real revival, then I don't know what it could be," remarked Billy after the Monday service. He added: "God is doing something here we have never seen before. I have a feeling that it is just beginning."

Commented the Rev. W. E. Sangster, Britain's best-known Methodist minister and pastor of Central Hall: "This is the nearest thing to Pentecost the world has ever seen."

The nearly 7,000 decisions in two nights equal the total of many four-week campaigns by Billy in the United States.

Unlike the opening service on Saturday when rain began to fall after the meeting began, the people on Monday knew what they faced. The rain began early in the afternoon and continued without letup as people jammed the subways and buses and splashed along on foot to the stadium. Part of the seats were under cover, but a majority sat out in the open. "I believe God has allowed this weather so Christians around the world will redouble their prayers," said Billy. He received a letter before the service saying that more people in Africa were praying for Wembley than for any event in history.

The people were already soaked when they rose to sing the opening song, "Blessed Assurance, Jesus Is Mine." They sang as if the stadium were flooded with bright sunshine. A holy hush seemed to settle over the vast throng as George Beverly Shea sang, "He's Got the Whole World in His Hands." Then all joined the 3,000 voice choir in singing the Twenty-third Psalm, "Goodness and Mercy, All my Life, Shall Surely Follow Me."

The great audience, composed in part by the best-dressed people in London, seemed to represent the rebirth of thinking described by world leaders as the only answer to the atomic bomb. Billy said, "Statistics show that ninety-five per cent of the people in the United States and ninety per cent in Great Britain believe in God. You ask, 'Isn't that enough?' No! The Bible says you can believe in God, you can believe in the Bible, you can believe in the church, and still miss the Kingdom of Heaven. The Bible says there has to come a moment when you surrender your life to Jesus Christ. Then you begin to live for Him, in the shop, in the office, in the school, and in the home." He asked, "Are you ready to do that?" Over 3,000 people walked out into the downpour and announced they were ready.

But an account of the biggest church news in 2,000 years was hard to find the next day in newspapers of the world's largest city. The pages were filled with the blow-by-blow happenings of a fist fight.

Ingenious Idea

THIS IS THE STORY OF AN INGENIOUS AMERICAN IDEA THAT mushroomed into the biggest project ever tackled by the post office in Great Britain. The idea, which began with scribbling on the back of an old envelope, made it possible for Evangelist Billy Graham to address unnumbered thousands each night in Scotland, England, Wales, and Ireland.

For lack of a better name it was labeled the Benninghoff Network—a special relay system over leased telephone lines. Over 2,500 cities, towns, and hamlets contracted for the service during the All-Scotland Crusade.

In one community, on an outlying island, the program relay from Kelvin Hall would have been interrupted if an emergency call for a doctor was necessary. The only telephone circuit carried the voice of Billy Graham with practically all the inhabitants listening over a loudspeaker.

Bob Benninghoff, a young engineer of the American Broadcasting Company, who handles all of Billy's "Hour of Decision" programs, conceived the idea at a prayer meeting during the first London crusade. It was probably the only prayer meeting he had ever attended. Bob isn't a member of the Graham team. "Their job is preaching," he said, "and mine is radio. I try to do my job."

There came a night during the London crusade when team members were assigned different hours to attend an all-night prayer meeting. One of the older members drew the 2:30 a.m. spot and it didn't seem right to Bob that he should be out that late alone. He said he would go along and keep the team member company. Bob sat uneasily on the back row of the strange surroundings and listened to the people pray. He noticed that the thing they prayed for most was more space to handle the people who wanted to hear Billy Graham. Thousands had to be turned away at the 12,000-seat Harringay Arena.

While the people prayed Bob pulled the used envelope out of his pocket and began to figure. The team member who was leading the meeting glanced toward the back row and gave him a disapproving glance because he seemingly was doodling on a scratch sheet while others prayed. The glance indicated that he could at least be respectful enough to bow his head. But Bob wasn't doodling. He was working on an idea that might solve the space problem. If people couldn't get into Harringay Arena, then why not take Harringay to the people with a loudspeaker relay? Such a private network had never before been tried on such a large scale, but that was no reason for not giving it a jolly good try, figured the transplanted engineer from Fort Wayne, Ind.

He approached the Graham team later and was given the green light to see what he could develop. Obstacles were ahead, however. He contacted post office officials in London. If this seems a little strange, the post office in Great Britain handles telephones as well as letters. Eyebrows went up all over the place when he revealed his plan, with one after another saying, "It has never been done, old boy." "Okay, so it's never been done," replied Bob. "Let's do it."

He finally was referred to an engineer named Archibald McKinley Middleton who had more imagination than his co-workers. He could visualize the possibility. Long notices had to be given to get regular lines, but he thought of the defense network used during World War II to alert cities that German bombers were on the way. It had been maintained in a standby status with virtually no use.

Just as things were looking up, another monkey wrench was thrown. A post office official said ninety-nine per cent of halls and churches in Great Britain were not equipped with connecting wires to feed loudspeakers and that such connections would take many months even if the materials could be obtained. Bob was still thinking. He asked if the halls and churches had telephones. Informed that they did, he said, "We can feed the loudspeakers through the telephone connection if we can get permission to temporarily disconnect the phone during the service." Again he was told, "It's never been done," and he gave his stock reply.

Only two or three points were connected for the first relay, but in forty-six days the requests climbed from less than five to over 400. In practically every location there was standing room only. One pastor reported that enterprising American servicemen tried to sell free tickets outside his church for one pound ($2.80). Thousands of people sat and listened to a loudspeaker and hundreds went forward to make decisions for Jesus Christ when Billy gave the invitation.

This destroyed the contention of many critics that Billy was successful only because of personal charm and mass emotionalism. These people haven't seen Billy Graham yet. Christian observers felt that the relay results were the greatest evidence of revival in Britain.

On one particular evening Bob was busily working his little patchwork radio station when a tube blew. Grabbing up scrap wires, he made hurried repairs and fed the network bare for anxious moments. He said, "There is absolutely no technical reason why all sound on the network didn't cease when the tube blew. But observers all along the line said it didn't go out. I don't understand it."

Bob, remember, isn't a member of the Graham team. More than faith and prayer, he prefers things he can put his finger on. After the success of the London venture, the post office began long-range planning for the All-Scotland Crusade, but the officials didn't visualize anything near 2,500 places requesting loudspeakers.

I recall the words of Bob one day during a bull session, after I had remarked, "It must make you feel awfully good to be directly responsible for so many people having an opportunity to accept Christ." "You know, George, it kind of scares me. Too many people could have killed the idea for this network but they didn't. Things happened that shouldn't have happened. I don't understand and it scares me." But as he said it I could tell it was a scared, wonderful feeling.

* * *

George Beverly Shea received a friendly letter of greeting from Helen Howarth Lemmell of Seattle, Wash., noted author of gospel hymns. She enclosed four lines of her most famous song, "Turn your eyes upon Jesus; Look full in His wonderful face. And the things of earth will grow strangely dim, In the light of His glory and grace."

Helen Lemmell is blind!

Animal Heaven

BILLY GRAHAM APPARENTLY BARKED UP THE WRONG FAMILY tree in a BBC broadcast.

He offended animal lovers throughout the United Kingdom and began ducking dog biscuits, fish food, and other assorted garbage thrown by supporters of "man's best friend."

It all started when Billy got up too early one day to appear on an early morning "Lift Up Your Hearts" program. He was too sleepy to realize the world-shaking significance of his remarks when he said, in illustrating a point, that:

"Fish belong to the sea, animals belong to the jungle, and human beings belong to God."

Then the animal kingdom began to roar, bark, bellow, meow, and scratch.

"Shocking and disgraceful" were the cries at the annual meeting in London of the League Against Cruel Sports.

Mrs. M. Dudley Ward of South Harrow asked animal lovers to support an open letter to Billy challenging him on this remark.

"We should tackle him on his own ground," she said, "for he never says a single word about our cause."

At the same meeting there were shouts of "good" when Lord Grey de Ruthyn announced that two of the jockeys riding in the Grand National were hurt. The lord reported that out of the thirty-one horses which started thirteen fell, thirteen finished, and five were pulled up exhausted.

Regarding the criticism, Billy was placed in good company. Mrs. G. Horsfall said she hoped that the Queen and Queen Mother would adopt a different attitude in the future and be on the side of mercy rather than take pleasure in attending anything so cruel as the Grand National. Lord Ruthyn said the Queen Mother's horse pulled up exhausted after completing one round.

Besieged in his hotel room, Billy announced that it had not been his intention to offend anyone, and he pointed out that his dog, "Belshazzar," was probably one of the biggest animals in North Carolina. He also owns a cat and a donkey.

All of the Grahams, he asserted, are very good to their pets.

Billy was too diplomatic to make the statement, but someone close to his organization remarked:

"Seems to me that the fish belong in the sea. Wouldn't it be cruel to take them all out?"

A London publication sent a woman writer to Glasgow for a serious article about Billy's views on pets. She cornered a member of his team, told him it was her belief that a special heaven existed for animals, and wanted to know why he didn't hold services for them.

With a straight face, he replied:

"I have been with Mr. Graham for several years and so far, to the best of my knowledge, all of his services have been for people. But if he decides to hold services for cats and dogs, I'll get in touch with you immediately."

She thanked him and left.

Billy wasn't at all prepared physically for the onslaught. He had just canceled an engagement to address the Glasgow Rotarians because of a cold and fever.

In an effort to fight off the ailment, he had been taking four different kinds of cold pills—red ones, blue ones, pink ones, and brown ones.

The doctor, after examining him, said: "You don't have any white pills."

So he gave him white ones!

Snow and Sleet

THIS ISN'T A WEATHER REPORT, BUT SNOW AND SLEET HIT London on a Tuesday night in May. The temperature dropped to thirty-seven degrees. Gales swept inland from the Atlantic. The 81,000-ton *Queen Mary* had to anchor off the Isle of Wight, while smaller ships raced for shelter. To quote a twentieth-century proverb, the weather was unusual.

It certainly wasn't any night to be holding a religious meeting in an outside arena where the elements fought each other for attention. But the incredible fact is that over 50,-000 people of London and surrounding area again went to Wembley Stadium and sat in the open for two hours to hear a preacher.

"We are seeing the greatest demonstration of spiritual hunger that I have ever witnessed," Billy said.

In appealing to Christians everywhere for even more prayer, Billy said: "We are keenly conscious that what we are witnessing in these days is fundamentally not man's work but God's. The breath of the Spirit of the Lord is sweeping across Britain and in our hearts is a consuming desire that 'He must increase, but we must decrease.' The message we proclaim is not one we devised, but it is the good news of the gospel. It was proclaimed by Roland Hill, John Wesley, George Whitfield, and hundreds of others. In essence it is simply this: Christ died for our sins, according to the Scriptures. The Bible says 'If we confess our sins, he is faithful and just to forgive us our sins, and to cleanse us from all unrighteousness.' "

*   *   *

Crusade Items and Quotes:

Two members of the Wembley Executive Committee made decisions for Christ during the Harringay meetings the previous year.

Crowd Appeal

IS THERE ANOTHER PERSON ON EARTH, BESIDES BILLY GRAHAM, who could attract 278,000 people on five nights? Think before ridiculing such a question. It might not be as foolish as you think.

The British admit that Sir Winston Churchill, greatest

orator of the twentieth century, couldn't do it. Marilyn
Monroe, with Liberace playing the piano for a torso tango,
couldn't do it. There isn't a single world leader or combination of politicians with that kind of crowd appeal. Russia's
Bulganin might possibly do it with command performances,
or five May Days in a row. There doesn't seem to be anyone
around with that kind of magic in his makeup.

But Billy Graham attracted such an incredible audience
in his first five nights at London's Wembley Stadium. The
people came in spite of rain, snow, sleet, and freezing winds.

At all attractions of the show world, the crowds dwindle
and the event closes. At Billy's campaigns, the crowds grow
with each appearance. He doesn't put on a show. Once the
services are under way, an associate evangelist reads from
the Bible, a soloist sings a hymn, a musical director leads the
choir in a church song, and then Billy speaks. A similar program can be heard in almost any church on any Sunday.

A logical question is: What's the answer? Billy has
held few press conferences in which puzzled reporters didn't
ask the question. And the reporters are seldom satisfied with
the answer they receive because they can't put it in a test
tube and analyze it. They can't put their fingers on the
answer and feel it.

"I have no logical explanation," says Billy. "I have been
told many times that I am just an ordinary preacher. I believe it. The only explanation is that this is God's doing and
not the work of a mere man. No one but the Spirit of God
could awaken such an interest in spiritual things, and we are
humbly grateful. The Bible says that if Jesus Christ be lifted
up He will draw all men unto Him. That is what we as a
team try to do—lift up Christ. I make every effort to stop
people from talking about Billy Graham and ask them to
lift up Christ."

Do the meetings attract any single class of people?

Stand outside and watch the crowds gather at any Graham rally and you will see people from all walks of life—taxi driver, housewife, businessman, politician. The Duchess of Kent from Britain's royal family attended a night service at Wembley. She snuggled deep in her seat to escape the cold winds, and cupped her chin in her hands as she listened intently. People sitting with her in the royal box said she intended telling the Queen all about her visit.

While the Queen was on a world tour, the Duke of Edinburgh wrote from Australia to a friend in England. He said they had heard much about this fellow Billy Graham and wanted to know more about him.

Is Billy Graham genuine? I have probably written more stories about Billy Graham than any other reporter alive. He is a better man off the platform than he is on it. His sincerity and humility affect the most bitter skeptics.

During the Harringay meetings here, England's most famous columnist, Cassandra, asked Billy to meet him on "sinners' ground." They met in a pub. Cassandra had beer. Billy had milk. And they talked. After the interview Cassandra retracted the disparaging things he had written about Billy, saying, "Sincerity and truth are weapons too sharp for me to oppose."

Queen Elizabeth Listens

A "GRACIOUS" QUEEN OF THE PEOPLE AND AN HUMBLE SERVANT of the King of kings had lunch together on Sunday after church.

Queen Elizabeth II and members of Great Britain's royal family were hosts to Dr. and Mrs. William Franklin Graham of Montreat, N. C.

And sometimes during the meal the man, who is known to millions around the world as "Billy," must have pinched himself to see if he was the same fellow who just a few years ago was milking cows on his father's dairy farm outside of Charlotte, N. C.

The occasion was a fitting climax to an incredible week. He had preached to 450,000 in Wembley Stadium and had seen 23,810 people walk onto the historic turf and take their stand for Christ. One of the men who stood there unashamedly in the drenching rain was Sir John Hunt, leader of the expedition that conquered Mt. Everest.

On Saturday Billy preached to 115,000. Sunday morning he preached the same "simple gospel" to less than 100 in a private chapel at Royal Lodge, Windsor Castle. No other American evangelist has ever been so honored.

Seated in the congregation were Queen Elizabeth, the Duke of Edinburgh, the Queen Mother, Princess Margaret, servants of the castle, and special invited guests. The children of the Queen and Duke were not present. Dr. Graham spoke approximately twenty-five minutes. An official announcement from the castle after the service stated:

"The Queen and Duke of Edinburgh today attended morning service in the private chapel at Royal Lodge, Windsor, at which the preacher was Dr. Billy Graham, the American evangelist. The Queen and Duke drove over from Windsor Castle, where they are in residence."

Reporters from several London newspapers, some of them lukewarm during the week but shocked to attention by the royal recognition, were waiting at the hotel when Dr. and Mrs. Graham returned at 3:30 p.m.

"It was a great privilege for me to speak at the service,"

he said. "The Queen was very charming and gracious." He confirmed the luncheon, told the length of his sermon, but refused to say when he had received the Queen's invitation.

In a previous article from Glasgow, I quoted an unidentified British statesman that Queen Elizabeth watched the evangelist on his Good Friday telecast from Kelvin Hall, along with 30,000,000 other viewers and listeners. The fact that the Queen did see the program was later confirmed. The invitation was presented shortly afterwards.

It is also believed that Princess Margaret attended services at Wembley incognito to escape recognition. She often wraps a scarf around her head and wipes away cosmetics, wandering unnoticed in crowds.

Dr. Graham told reporters that he used Acts 27:25 as the text for his sermon. He declined to elaborate. Shortly before he left the United States for the campaigns abroad he spoke before President and Mrs. Eisenhower in the National Presbyterian Church, Washington, D. C. The text on that occasion was the same—Acts 27:25, which says, "Wherefore, sirs, be of good cheer: for I believe God, that it shall be even as it was told me."

The following statements were made during the sermon before President Eisenhower. Illustrations and sequence vary, but in essence the sermon is the same as the one delivered before Queen Elizabeth. He said:

". . . The Apostle Paul was going from one city to another preaching one message—Jesus Christ and Him crucified. He was on a ship when a storm arose. The ship was being tossed about by the wind and waves. The men were frightened. Paul went to his room and prayed. When he came out, his face glowed with a look of peace and assurance as he made this statement: 'Be of good cheer, I believe God.'

"There are many storms in the world today. There are storms of atheism, materialism, internationalism. Homes are broken. Juvenile delinquency is rampant. Crimes are on the increase. There are other storms in the personal life of people —storms of discouragements, bereavements, confusions, frustrations. But Paul said, 'Have faith, be of good cheer.'

"Faith is probably the most important word in the New Testament. It is mentioned ninety-two times in the Book of John. It is so important that God said unless you have the right kind of faith you can't get to heaven. Faith is taking God at His word. . . ."

Presbyterians Honor Baptist

BILLY, AN ORDAINED MINISTER OF THE SOUTHERN BAPTIST Convention, was given a foot-stomping ovation in Edinburgh, Scotland, amid pomp and pageantry at the Presbyterian General Assembly, following the conclusion of his Wembley meetings.

He had been invited to attend the assembly as special guest of the Duke of Hamilton, Lord High Commissioner and cousin of the Queen, and was given quarters in Holy-rood Palace.

In the usual course of events, as people in the United States well know, Presbyterians just don't go around doing things like that for Baptists. But Billy seems to have broken across practically all denominational lines.

The North Carolina preacher addressed the assembly briefly, saying:

"The essence of any evangelism is prayer, unity, and

the teaching of the gospel of the Lord Jesus Christ. We give thanks to God and to you for your tolerance and sympathetic understanding, your co-operation and your prayers, God bless you and thank you very much."

The Rev. D. P. Thomson, one of the leaders of the Tell Scotland movement, asked the assembly "to give thanks to God for the work accomplished through His servant, Dr. Billy Graham." He said he was not asking the assembly to endorse Dr. Graham's theology, or his methods, or his views about anything.

"But I do ask you to say this," he said, "Dr. Graham has been God's messenger to us at this time."

Thunderous applause followed the remark. Billy sat with his head bowed.

* * *

Billy rented some special formal clothes for his short stay at Holyrood Castle.

"Never in my life have I seen so many top hats and striped trousers," he commented later. "I turned to one of the perfectly attired men at a banquet and said, 'Your grace, I don't believe we've met.' He replied, 'I'm your waiter, sir.'"

* * *

Dr. Paul Maddox, chief of chaplains in the European theater during World War II, was visiting London one day in 1946 and heard that a young American preacher named Billy Graham was to speak at a church that night. He attended the service.

Afterwards he was so enthusiastic over the man and his message that he had his wife come over from Germany to hear him. As they sat in the congregation, Dr. Maddox overheard a remark from a couple in the next seat.

"I wish all of England could hear this young minister," said the man to his wife.

This wish came true.

Dr. Maddox is now a special aide to the young preacher he heard in 1946.

*   *   *

A good-looking young Englishman was mad at Billy Graham for months after his girl friend was converted at a meeting in Harringay Arena. He couldn't adapt his life to her new way of thinking and a split-up followed.

The Englishman grew more bitter with the passing months and when Billy held a press conference in London, he planned with a photographer to humiliate the evangelist. The plan was that as soon as Billy got up to speak, the Englishman would walk up, slap him, and the picture would be blazoned on the front page next day. But when Billy arose, the Englishman stayed in his seat. "Go ahead," said the photographer. But the man refused, saying he "just couldn't do it."

Several days later, during a Saturday afternoon service at Wembley Stadium, the young Englishman walked down from the stands when the invitation was given and took his place before the platform with hundreds of others making decisions for Jesus Christ.

The story might sound better if he was reunited with his girl, but such is not the case. She is married to another.

He is no longer bitter, however. I had lunch with him one day and he remarked:

"How is it possible for one to overlook such a wonderful experience as this for so long?" And he smiled happily as he said it.

Songs and Stories

INTERESTING STORIES ARE OFTEN CONNECTED WITH GOSPEL songs.

Bev Shea was strolling with his wife, little boy, and friends at the Chelsea Flower Show in London. A man walked up, introduced himself, and said he had been converted the previous year at the Harringay meetings.

As they chatted, the man told Bev about a friend of his who had gone to Harringay in order to scoff. He made fun of everything connected with the meeting.

"But when you got to the part of your song in which you held out your arms and sang, 'He's got that wee tiny baby in his hands,' it melted the heart of my friend and he found Christ," related the man.

Here is a story about the way in which a gospel song was written:

Several years ago when Billy Graham was holding a campaign in California, one of the men who made a decision was Stuart Hamblen. He was a popular entertainer, with a radio program, and owned a string of race horses. But the Lord spoke to his heart and he gave up the things of the world to serve Christ. He witnessed at every opportunity and wrote songs about the Saviour.

One day he was walking along the street in Hollywood when he bumped into an old friend of his, John Wayne, the movie star.

"I have been hearing about this change in your life, Stuart," Wayne said and asked, "What's it all about?"

"It is no secret what God can do," replied Stuart.

"Say, that sounds like the title to a song," Wayne said.

And it was, only the song hadn't been written. The thought stayed with Stuart until he wrote the song that is now well loved, especially in America.

"I'd Rather Have Jesus," is the song Bev Shea sings as his own testimony.

He was a young man and having difficulties in his Christian life. Worldly opportunities were opening up, but he couldn't feel right in his heart that this was the work God wanted him to do. There were opportunities on the stage and in radio.

Bev's mother knew that he was doing a lot of serious thinking. She also knew that he had a habit of sitting down at the piano for a few minutes every Sunday morning before church.

She had found the words to a little poem and placed them on the piano, where he would be sure to see them. He walked into the living room, read the words, and immediately without stopping wrote the music for "I'd Rather Have Jesus." That same morning he sang the song for the first time at the church next door, where his father was the pastor.

The song has been a constant reminder that he'd "rather have Jesus than silver or gold . . . or men's applause."

One of the most inspiring stories I have ever heard concerns Bev's friend, Burt Frizen, who lives in Wheaton, Ill.

Burt has a wonderful baritone voice. His mother also loved to sing. While he was still a youngster she taught him the song, "Jesus Whispers Peace."

Then came World War II and Burt was fighting in the Battle of the Bulge. He was badly injured and unable to make his way to safety. For six hours he lay out on the battle-field, waiting for death or whatever was to come.

Much of the time he sang softly, over and over again, the words to the song he had learned from his mother—"there is a name to me most dear . . . like sweetest music to my ear . . . for when my heart is troubled, filled with fear . . . Jesus whispers peace."

Hearing a sound nearby, he opened his eyes and saw a German soldier standing over him with a gun.

"This is it," thought Burt as he waited for the shot.

But the German didn't shoot. He said, "Sing it again."

As Burt began to sing the song again he felt the German lift him in strong arms and place him on the ledge of a rock.

His own medics spotted him a few minutes later and took him to safety.

Jesus had whispered peace in the midst of violent war.

Mr. Churchill and Dr. Graham

WHAT DID SIR WINSTON CHURCHILL, THE STATESMAN, SAY to Billy Graham, the evangelist?

It may never be known what Sir Winston said to Billy when the two met privately for forty minutes at No. 10 Downing Street during the first London crusade. The question is still unanswered a year later.

The aged diplomat, now retired and feeble in everything except the great voice and keen mind, asked Billy to keep the talk confidential. The request has been respected.

But it doesn't take a genius to figure out what Billy said to Sir Winston. Any person who knows Billy well is aware of the fact that he doesn't compromise the message of Christ, which he has presented to the high and the low at every opportunity. It has been the same to lords and ladies, to the masses, to leaders of government, to the Archbishop of Canterbury.

And he didn't mellow the message when talking with Mr. Churchill.

Billy told the man generally regarded as the world's greatest statesman that Jesus Christ, not statesmanship, was the only answer for the overwhelming problems facing the world.

He told Mr. Churchill that sin in the heart of man, not Russia, was the biggest danger to world security . . . that the atom bomb hadn't made itself and wouldn't set itself off.

He told him that a man must be born again to enter the Kingdom of God. Then he presented the simple plan of salvation through faith in Christ.

Billy could have told Sir Winston what American statesmen had said. But he didn't. He told him what the Bible said.

On the night before his talk with Mr. Churchill, Billy and members of his team did more of the same kind of witnessing in high places. They were guests of honor at a banquet given by Lord and Lady Luke in the ballroom of the Dorchester Hotel.

Everything was ultra formal, with evening gowns and tails. Titles were a shilling a dozen. About 250 people were present.

A lady sitting across the table from Grady Wilson was hard of hearing. She asked, in a loud voice:

"Ah, Mr. Wilson, what takes place, you know, when those people are taken inside that place you call a counseling room?"

Grady breathed a sigh of thankfulness for such an opportunity. Naturally, he had to talk a little loud, since she was hard of hearing, and the others nearby couldn't help listening to the remarks:

"The first thing we tell them is that all have sinned—that it doesn't make any difference who they are, from the lowest servant to the highest of nobility. Then we tell them that they can't save themselves. Only Jesus Christ can do that. After this the people are told they must surrender their lives to Christ and trust Him. Once the primary decision has been made, we urge them to read their Bibles every day, to pray, witness, and get active in a church."

After the diners had finished eating, Lord Luke called on Billy for a few words. Attention was undivided as he spoke.

The guests filed out of the dining room in a thoughtful mood.

"His success is not showmanship; it is sincerity," said Sir David Eccles, then Minister of Works.

"Now I understand," commented Mrs. Neville Chamberlain, widow of the former Prime Minister.

Sodom on the Seine

PARIS, SOMETIMES REFERRED TO AS SODOM ON THE SEINE, probably figured it could take Billy Graham in its devil-may-care stride.

But it couldn't! Things happened, from start to finish.

The campaign, sponsored by Alliance Evangelique Francaise, was the first major Protestant evangelistic effort for France in modern history. Pastor Jean P. Benoit was the chairman. Scores of counselors were trained and a choir of 400 rehearsed French songs for several days under the direction of Cliff Barrows and Dave Barnes of the European Bible Institute. It was not an easy job to find 400 hymn singers in Paris. Glasgow had 4,000.

George Beverly Shea put in long hours studying the tricky French phrasing, so that people could understand his gospel tunes. Pianist Tedd Smith and Organist Paul Meckelson were lucky. Their instruments speak all languages.

Billy Graham, fortified by a brief sun-kissed holiday in Italy and the courage of his convictions, was greeted at the railway station by 200 Parisians singing "Blessed Assurance" in French.

Another person who greeted him at the railway station was a special officer assigned by the Prefect of Police for the duration of his stay. This is an honor usually reserved for top-ranking diplomats.

Next day Billy faced the Paris press which turned out in large numbers. The reporters had fed him to the wolves a year before because of a story in which he was quoted as saying that "France is like a watch without its mainspring. It has run down."

In his opening remarks at the press conference he referred to the incident, saying:

"In Germany last year I was asked by a reporter what I thought of France. I told him many wonderful things about France, but in the conversation I quoted the remarks of a diplomat from the Far East. The quote was the only thing he used. I regret it very much."

The subject was not brought up again at the press conference. Biggest question in the minds of the reporters was wrapped around the thought: "Are you here to lead an anti-Catholic crusade?" Billy's reply: "I am not in France to lead an anti-Catholic crusade. I am here to preach Christ as the only hope of the world. I am here to tell the people of France what the Bible has to say. It is our hope that a spiritual revolution will create a third force in the world—a force that will not be appeasement or war, but will be a Christian force that people on both sides of the Iron Curtain will accept."

Here are some of the questions and answers:

Question: If Catholics make decisions at your meetings will you encourage them to return to the faith they were born into?

Answer: My objective is to get the people to accept Jesus Christ. The names of converts will be turned over to the Evangelistic Alliance which invited us to France.

Question: Are there any Catholic members of the Alliance?

Answer: No. (A member of the Alliance interrupted to say that cards of people requesting reaffirmation in the Catholic faith would be turned over to the Catholic church.)

Question: Is this your first series of meetings in a country predominantly Catholic?

Answer: Yes.

Question: Why have you not gone to Italy for meetings?
Answer: We haven't been invited.

Question: Will you speak through an interpreter?

Answer: Yes. But I have found the message gains through interpretation. It gives the people time to think.

Question: You said you would not answer questions about politics. Don't you think there is a connection between religion and politics?

Answer: There is an indirect connection. We cannot have a better world without better men. Men changed by the transforming power of Jesus Christ can go out and make a moral and social impact on the world. In that way there is a connection.

Question: Aren't you afraid that a decision made in minutes will not last?

Answer: When I met my wife, I decided in less than five minutes that I wanted to marry her. Wars have been started in less than five minutes. *Reader's Digest* picked 100 names at random of people who made decisions at Harringay in London. They found only one person who said he didn't mean it.

Question: (From a French female reporter) Do you always bring (handsome) Cliff Barrows with you?

Answer: Yes.

And so it went.

Lack of Faith

BILLY GRAHAM WAS RELAXING IN A SMALL CURTAINED ROOM underneath the stands at the Velodrome d'Hiver (winter bicycle arena).

He was a happy man!

People had warned that the Paris meeting, his first extended campaign in a non-English speaking, predominantly Catholic nation, would be his Waterloo. It had begun as one of his greatest successes.

As he sat in the dressing room, he was still a bit awed by what he had just seen at the opening Sunday night meeting attended by 9,645.

"I just didn't have enough faith to believe that God would do what we have seen tonight," he said. "I had prayed for 100 decisions so that Christians here would be encouraged. There must have been nearly 600 who walked down the aisles and they meant business. I have never seen such earnest prayers in the counseling room."

Speaking through an interpreter in short rapid phrases, Billy preached on "The Cross of Jesus Christ" and then gave an invitation for people to walk forward and surrender their lives.

The response was instantaneous. There had been anxious moments of hesitation at the first meeting of the All-Scotland Crusade, but this was not the case in supposedly indifferent Paris. In less than thirty seconds, people were standing at the front and they continued to come without letup as the 400 voice choir sang softly. Billy stood silently on the platform with arms folded and waited. The simple message had reached a strange assortment of people.

Sprinkled in with the scores of Frenchmen moving forward were Chinese, Mexicans, Negroes, Americans, Germans, Spaniards, and others from practically every country in Europe. Paris is a melting pot.

Billy has often stated in his messages that people may speak different languages but that the longings of their souls are the same. It appeared that ninety per cent of those making decisions were adults, many of them sixty or seventy years of age. Young couples joined hands as they moved to the platform. Mothers and fathers brought their children. Most were well dressed. A variety of costumes indicated various faiths. The evangelist had said in his talk: "I am not asking you to join any particular church. I am asking you to surrender your lives to Christ. You may be a member of the church and have a form of religion, but Jesus said you must be born again. Have you been born again? Are you sure of it? If you haven't, you will never get to heaven, no matter who you are."

One of those taking her stand at the front was a beautiful Mexican actress in Paris to make a movie. She had been in the congregation when Billy spoke on Sunday morning to a packed throng including diplomats and Hollywood stars at the American Cathedral. After the service she had gripped his hand and said, "When you give the invitation tonight I am going to be among those making decisions."

The crowds began arriving early for the evening service at the arena, located near the Eiffel Tower. A bus-load of American airmen drove 150 miles to attend.

French papers said that the capacity of the Velodrome is 20,000. But in the throng of 9,645, people had to stand in the aisles.

It is doubtful if any religious meeting has ever been held under more confusing circumstances. Everything seemed to go wrong. The microphones were not functioning properly and the press was having its problems. A French official had reserved seats for French writers, leaving a number of American writers and broadcasters to shift for themselves. Over all the confusion was the babble of excitable Parisians who love to talk, and do in torrents.

The complicated task of having all directions interpreted added to the chaos as Cliff Barrows got the program under way with congregational hymns. In the mixups, half the people would be standing and half sitting. Then they would reverse. A bewildered technician kept turning lights on and off in varied combinations. Another minor official shouted several times across the hall at someone in an effort to give directions, but never made his point.

There were enough cameras on hand to film "The Birth of A Nation." In the middle of a talk by the campaign chairman, a man wandered up on the stage and began adjusting mikes.

A resemblance to order had been achieved by the time Billy arose to speak, and the people grew quiet as he began to give them simple explanations from the Bible for everyday problems and matters of eternal life.

The people seemed hungry to hear him!

* * *

Billy Graham's European tour was organized and directed by Bob Evans, an old classmate from Wheaton College who has done a magnificent job in founding and expanding the European Bible Institute at Paris. Graduating students spread from the school throughout Europe to do evangelistic work in their own countries.

Bob went to a small town once in the interior of Europe to preach. As he approached the door of the church, an old man stopped him, pulled a faded piece of paper from his inside pocket and asked:

"Mister, can you tell me what book this page came from?"

Bob looked at the page and exclaimed:

"This is a page from the Bible, sir."

The old man looked at it lovingly before replying:

"I have read this page over and over for many years. I didn't know where it came from, but I knew in my heart there was something different about these words."

Bob had the pleasure of giving him a Bible—the first that the old man had ever seen.

Puddles of Chaos

ABILITY TO THINK ON THE FEET IS A RARE ASSET.

Evangelist Billy Graham was in the middle of his address at the Velodrome d'Hiver. Attention of the 6,000 was riveted on the platform from where the smartly dressed young preacher was ricocheting explosive Bible bullets off the lips of his French interpreter.

Then he almost lost the audience.

Lightning flashed outside the huge arena and rain began to beat a sharp tattoo on the roof.

This in itself was not very unusual, but someone had neglected to close a big skylight and torrents of water came down through the opening to give the excited Parisians an unscheduled baptizing.

In Great Britain, where rain falls on one side of a house and the sun shines on the other, the water would have gone unnoticed. The disciplined Britons would have put up their ever-ready umbrellas and gone on listening.

But no one ever accused the French of being disciplined. When the rain came through the skylight, they began to scatter. A fat woman began climbing over seats and lost one of her shoes in the process. A news photographer with fast reflexes caught her in the undignified position as she pulled her pounds over the hazardous short-cut.

Someone clambered up to the roof and closed the skylight before complete pandemonium broke loose, but no sooner had this been done than little puddles of chaos began popping up all over the arena.

To coin a phrase, the roof leaked like a sieve, and there wasn't a pan in the house. People sitting in direct lines of fire began shifting to other localities.

The arena normally is used for bicycle races, but the bikes were not running this night. People were!

Billy handled it deftly. Almost without breaking stride he smiled and said, "The God I have been talking about is the One who brings the rain. God uses the rain to make flowers grow and to help the farmers grow food from the earth. I grew up on a farm down in North Carolina and sometimes, when it wouldn't rain for long spells, we wouldn't have enough to eat. I never complain about the rain but thank God for helping the farmers.

"The same God who brings this rain loved you enough to send His Son, Jesus Christ, to die on the cross for your sins."

He was back into the heart of his message and the attention of the audience had been recaptured.

❊　　❊　　❊

Paris Items:

Col. William D. Kirkpatrick of Waxahachie, Tex., chaplain of the U. S. European command, said he spotted about seventy-five American servicemen from all over France at one service. A spiritual awakening is under way in the armed forces, he said. . . . "This is just like Easter," announced the Very Rev. Sturgis Lee Riddle, Dean of the American Cathedral in Paris, at the Sunday morning service when the Episcopal Church was jammed for guest speaker Billy Graham. . . . A Russian visited Billy at his hotel and said people were praying in Russia for the Paris meetings.

They Couldn't Wait

BILLY GRAHAM HAD JUST FINISHED A MESSAGE IN WHICH HE compared the idolatry of modern Paris with ancient Athens.

"Anything that takes more of your time than you give to God is an idol, and God hates idolatry," he stated in the talk.

Now he was in the process of giving an invitation for people to renounce sin and turn by faith to Jesus Christ.

But four persons didn't give him time to finish. They arose from their seats in different sections of the Velodrome and walked to the platform before the appeal was given.

The first to go was a middle-aged Frenchman. He walked down before 8,080 with shoulders erect and head held high as if he had waited all his life to find peace with God and couldn't wait another minute. A woman joined him. Two men left their seats.

Sensing the mood of the crowd Billy quickly finished the appeal and invited others to take their stand for Christ. Streams of people representing several nationalities poured forward.

The Bible had been explained in a way they could understand, with a French pastor relaying the words of the young American. A boy with a crew cut stepped down the aisle, followed by a sophisticated woman. A woman in a wheel chair was pushed forward by a friend. People came from all directions . . . two French soldiers, a man humped with age, a girl in pigtails, an elderly white-headed woman, who walked with the aid of a cane, a mother with twin teen-agers, a young beauty with a French hair-do.

It had to be the message that brought them. No man could appeal to so many different types and ages.

Nothing like this had ever happened before in Paris, supposedly the most indifferent city on earth to the Bible. "I never thought I would live to see this," said one pastor. "We are seeing a miracle in Paris," commented Billy in his message.

The evangelist drew a parallel between Paris and Athens, where the Apostle Paul stood on Mars Hill and preached a sermon on the unknown God. "Thousands of you sitting here tonight are religious," Billy said, "but your God is not real to you. He is unknown."

He added: "One of the groups that listened to Paul was known as the Epicureans. These people thought God was a kind old man sitting around on a cloud who loved people too much to judge them. This is a false idea of God. He hates sin. Epicureans said that here and now was all that mattered, so let's eat, drink, and be merry. Many of you are the same. This path leads to destruction. Another group that listened to Paul was the Stoics. They were the proud intellectuals who thought they were too smart for God. To them God and the Bible were laughable. They didn't need Him. Their time was filled with the discussion of great philosophical questions. They could reason their way to God if it became necessary. I want to tell you this: Any God you can put in a test tube and measure is not the true God. To find God you must humble yourself and become as a child. Your intellect will never get you to heaven, I don't care who you are. Unless you repent you will perish. Billy Graham didn't say that. God said it."

He reminded the listeners of three reactions that day on Mars Hill.

"A majority of the people laughed at Paul. They mocked him and his God. Scores of them decided to delay the matter—they would hear him again at another season. Many never did and neither will you. A few of the people believed and followed Christ. All three reactions are present here again in Paris tonight.

"What is your reaction?"

Hollywood to Paris

THE PRETTY WIFE OF A HOLLYWOOD TELEVISION EXECUTIVE beamed as she sat in the counseling room of the Velodrome d'Hiver.

A few minutes before she had walked to the front of the arena with 457 others when Evangelist Billy Graham had finished speaking to the crowd of 10,000 and had given an invitation for all to accept Christ.

"Just think," remarked the young woman, "I had to come from Hollywood to Paris to find Christ." She and her husband were on a tour of Europe and decided to accept the invitation of friends to attend one of the Graham meetings.

Other notables in the congregation the same evening included Sir Gladwyn Jebb, British Ambassador to France, and Wallace Haines, a member of the International Council of Christian Leadership, who brought three young countesses with him.

The meetings in Paris, however, were not aimed exclusively at the smart international set. Walking down the same aisle with the Hollywood matron was a tough youngster from the back streets of Paris and a poorly dressed woman whose appearance showed she had put in long hours of back-breaking work.

"I have felt the same hunger here for Christ that I felt in London," Billy said. "This city can be won for Christ and the results will be felt around the world."

It was impossible to engage the Velodrome, largest indoor arena in France, for more than five days at this particular season. But Billy has expressed an interest in returning to Paris for a long engagement in the future. The handful of Protestants in Paris, who have seen what can be accomplished, already are making plans for a bigger and better crusade.

*   *   *

Billy, who learned to cope as a driver with the madcap road standards in preparation for his European tour by car, was behind the wheel one day as he circled the Arch of Triumph.

France's "Unknown Soldier" is buried under the arch and the quickest way for a pedestrian to join him permanently is to attempt a foot crossing, with wild Parisian drivers shooting in all directions.

Billy spotted a walker, braked his car to a stop, and smiled as he motioned the pedestrian across. The fellow was so startled that he stopped in front of the car and stared. Courteous drivers in France just aren't to be found. A civic group planned to give a prize to the most courteous cab driver but called the whole thing off. They couldn't find one.

*   *   *

A Paris magazine, describing Billy as "inventor of the technology of salvation," pushed its imagination to the limit in describing his campaigns in America, saying: "Billy Graham makes his entry to a city, with his main staff of preachers preceding in a caravan. The Cadillac of Billy Graham (he doesn't own one) follows, while the crowd throws out confetti on his way or waves flags in his honor. Abroad his methods are more modest." Everybody, it seems, loves a parade, even if it has to be imagined.

* * *

One of Billy's pet peeves is the man who thinks a person has to be long-faced to be a Christian. "I met a man in New York once and he had the longest, saddest face I have ever seen on a human being. I asked him why he appeared so sad and he said, 'I'm a Christian.' A Christian is the only person in the world who has anything to be happy about. He has peace and assurance in his heart and should greet people with a smile."

* * *

People are always asking Billy if the converts at the meetings last, and he replies: "Some of them won't, but many will. The Bible teaches that. There were 400 who accepted Christ in Charlotte, N. C. the same night I did twenty years ago. I know of five ministers today who came from that group. I know many outstanding businessmen who stood there that night and they are still living Christian lives."

A Change of Mind

Dr. Marc Boegner is known in his native France as "Mr. Protestant."

His voice carries weight and authority. The people look to him for leadership.

The influence of Dr. Boegner carries far beyond the boundaries of France. He is a past president of the World Council of Churches.

When ministers of Paris were planning the campaign of Billy Graham for the French capital, they asked the Protestant leader to join the committee. They had never attempted a crusade of such magnitude and the prestige of Dr. Boegner was eagerly sought.

But "Mr. Protestant" wasn't having any. He would not lend his name to the meetings of the American evangelist.

The five-day crusade was held anyway and was successful beyond all expectations.

Dr. Boegner did not attend a single service.

A man and wife who made decisions at one of the meetings, in filling out the questionnaire card to take advantage of follow-up instruction, wrote in the name of Dr. Boegner as the pastor they wanted to receive the card. This was a bit unusual. He hadn't been pastor of a church for several years, while devoting his time to inter-church work.

After receiving the card, he scratched his memory and recalled the couple. They had attended the last church of which he had been pastor.

"They attended faithfully, but really weren't very good members," he related. "They never had any real interest in the church."

Dr. Boegner was curious to see the effect on the lives of the man and wife. He decided to call on them and see for himself.

"I was transfixed as soon as the door was opened at the home," he commented later. "The people in this home were different from the ones I remembered. They had a glow on their faces that came from the heart.

"During the forty-five minutes I was in the house, I didn't talk to them about God. They talked to me about Him and what He had done in their lives."

Dr. Boegner told the story several weeks after the end of the crusade, when he attended a testimony meeting of over 1,000 persons who had made decisions after hearing Billy.

Shortly before the meeting was scheduled to end, "Mr. Protestant" rose to his feet at the rear of the hall and said:

"I didn't take any part in the campaign, but I'm sorry that I didn't. I have been shown very clearly that the decisions were real and I believe they will be lasting. I want to state in public that if Dr. Billy Graham returns to Paris for a campaign, I will be privileged and happy to support the meetings in any way possible."

The doubts had been dissolved. A formerly indifferent man and wife had written down the name of a pastor who didn't have a church.

A Suicide Pact

THIS IS A TRUE STORY THAT HAPPENED TWO WEEKS BEFORE IT was written.

It was a remarkable story when first heard, but it just wasn't right to tell it, as you will understand after reading. And the facts needed checking.

Two young French art students had made a suicide pact. The young men had rationalized life down to the dreary point where it had no real meaning for them. They had tried everything life had to offer, with all the gay trimmings of wine, women, and song, but it had ended in an emotional hangover.

They picked an evening for the last event in their lives. The method was to be by drowning in the Seine River at Paris. They collected heavy weights to hold their bodies under water. The meeting place, for no particular reason, was to be in front of the Velodrome d'Hiver. One of the young men was there at the appointed time. He paced up and down for long, anxious minutes as he waited for his friend. A lot of people were going inside the arena, where a poster out front proclaimed the appearance of an American named Billy Graham. Tiring of the wait, he decided to go inside and see what was happening.

He heard the evangelist as he told the story of Jesus Christ. And he listened to the words: "Christ can lift every burden and He will put a new spring in your step. Invite Him into your heart and He will give you a new life that has joyous meaning and purpose."

The art student was among several hundred who walked forward at the invitation to try this strange, new way of life.

Along with the others he bowed his head and prayed, repeating the words after Billy: "Oh, God, I'm a sinner. I confess my sin. I renounce my sin. I believe Jesus Christ died so that my sin could be forgiven. And by faith I receive Christ as Lord, Master, and Saviour."

There was a new sparkle in the youth's eyes when he had finished the prayer. His first thought was for his friend and he rushed outside to tell him what had happened. The friend couldn't be found. He searched all over the area, sick with the thought that he might have gone through with the plan.

And this was the status of the story when it was first told by Dr. J. A. Blocher, head of the Nogent Bible School in Paris, who served as interpreter for Billy during his meetings in the French capital.

I later met Dr. Blocher in Geneva and asked him whether the art student had found his friend. And the distinguished-looking French professor beamed as he answered:

"Yes, he found him a few days later and is now doing his best to win him for Christ. I had a talk with the one who attended the meeting and he verified all points in the story. In my opinion there is no doubt that he found a new life on the night he planned to destroy himself."

Hitler's Children

TEN YEARS AGO THE GERMAN CITY OF FRANKFURT WAS DEAD, demoralized, and beaten.

Rains of Allied bombs had practically leveled three-fourths of the homes, stores, and plants. But the Germans rolled up their hearts and went to work.

Today it is difficult to determine that Frankfurt was almost blasted from the earth. The hum of building is evident everywhere in the bustling city. The city, however, did not keep pace spiritually.

The spiritual needs got a big boost when Billy Graham held a one-night meeting in Frankfurt Stadium. An estimated 35,000 were present. Billy's message was the same that brought such incredible responses in Glasgow, London, Paris, Zurich, and Geneva.

When the invitation was given, lines of smartly uniformed German boys formed paths across the track to the green turf. Ten years ago these boys were known as Hitler's children and knew no God save the Führer.

People streamed through the lanes and then kept coming in greater numbers. A customs official, who had been watching the radio equipment, left his post and joined them. The silent procession lasted almost thirty minutes. There appeared to be over 3,000 standing in front of the platform. They had heard the young man and believed his message:

"Jesus Christ is the way, the truth, and the life."

*   *   *

John Bolton, once a close acquaintance of Adolf Hitler and now a director of several United States business firms, was the first man who asked Billy Graham to preach in Germany.

Several years ago he asked Billy to take the message of Christ to his former countrymen. Bolton, who split with Hitler after the German leader began his godless rise to power, flew from America to attend several of the European meetings held by Billy. He gave the benediction at several.

A Wonderful Afternoon

BILLY GRAHAM'S AFTERNOON HAD BEEN FULL AND EXCITING. At 1:00 p.m., as guest of Lt. Gen. William H. Tunney, commander-in-chief of the U. S. Air Forces in Europe, he had addressed 5,000 Americans and Germans at Wiesbaden. But he tarried too long at the air base. With a long ride ahead, he was to speak at 4:00 p.m. at the Kaiserslautern base, largest American community outside the United States.

Cliff Barrows, Bev Shea, and Tedd Smith had gone ahead to play safe. It was a good move, because 8,000 Army personnel were on hand and Billy was late. Bev stalled by singing a number of old favorite hymns. The soldiers and officers knew he was stalling, but they were too busy listening to be restless.

At 4:20 p.m. Billy's car came roaring up. A military escort had led him on a wild ninety-mile-an-hour ride through the German countryside. At both camps, Billy urged the servicemen to be ambassadors for Jesus Christ as well as for the United States. He said: "You have a responsibility of living a life of honesty, integrity, and morality in front of these people."

In a straight-from-the-shoulder message, he told the GI's:

"The Christian life isn't long-faced. It's wonderful and deep down in your soul you are longing for the peace that only Christ can give. Your buddies in the barracks may not know it, but you know it."

He asked the men to indicate their desire to follow Christ by raising their hands. Hundreds did so, including many officers sitting on the platform.

That should have been enough excitement for one afternoon, but the best was still to come, unplanned and unrehearsed.

With his wife and a few friends, Billy was motoring back to his hotel at Heidelberg when he noticed that the route passed through Worms, one of the oldest towns in Europe.

Worms has been settled without interruption since the younger Stone Age, 2500 B.C. It is older than Rome.

The evangelist expressed a desire to stop and see the statue of Martin Luther and other leaders of the Protestant Reformation. It was at the Diet of Worms in 1521 that Luther appeared before a galaxy presided over by Emperor Charles V and was asked to recant his famous papers. This, in part, was his reply:

"My conscience is captive to the Word of God. I cannot and I will not recant anything, for to go against conscience is neither right nor safe. Here I stand. I cannot do otherwise, God help me, Amen."

Billy gazed thoughtfully at the words on the base of Luther's statue and he glanced at four other statues surrounding the central figure. They were of other leaders of the Reformation, Waldus (French), Wyclif (English), Hus (Czech), and Savonarola (Italian).

Someone in the small groups wandering around the Protestant shrine recognized the tall young American.

"Billy Graham is here," was the word that spread like wildfire through the scattered couples. Practically all of them produced Bibles or Testaments and asked him to write his name in them. One man explained that a number of those present were members of Christian Railmen's Association and asked if they could sing a song for Billy.

As they began to sing, people were attracted by the music and the word spread farther that Billy was at the statue of Luther. People could be seen running down the surrounding streets. As they arrived at the statue, they joined the singers, who formed a semi-circle around Billy. It wasn't only what they sang that was inspiring. It was the expressions on the faces of the people.

They loved this American they had never seen, and wanted him to know it. He was not a Luther, but he was doing his best to do what he could. Billy's wife, Ruth, stood off at the side and couldn't hold back the tears. Then Bev sang a song, "Gentle Saviour," in German, for the people who had gathered. All of the people wanted to talk with Billy and he wanted to talk with them, but there was a language barrier and the words could not be understood. In spite of the barrier, however, there was a bond of love in Christ on both sides.

Billy was thoughtful as he drove away from Worms and the waving people. He had lived a wonderful afternoon.

Question and Answer

A FEW OF THE WRITERS WERE GIVING BILLY GRAHAM "THE business" at a press conference in Mannheim, a German city reported by authorities to have the strongest concentration of Communists outside the Iron Curtain.

One reporter asked:

"What do you know about the suffering of Christ that you preach about so often? You have never suffered. You live well and have the comforts of life."

And Billy answered:

"When a Western Union messenger boy delivers a death message to a home he doesn't take part in all the suffering connected with the message. He just delivers the telegram. That's all I am—God's messenger boy. I don't ask that people look up to Billy Graham. I ask them to respect Jesus Christ. I didn't die on a cross. Neither did you. But Christ did. He suffered and died for your sins. I hope you will be at the meeting tonight."

The heckling reporter may not have been present, but over 40,000 other Germans and Americans overflowed Mannheim Stadium. Occupying a special box was Gen. Anthony C. McAuliffe, commander of all U. S. armed forces in Europe. Gen. McAuliffe was the man who rose to fame on one word, "Nuts" to the German surrender demand at Bastogne.

Some members of the throng gathered at 10:30 a.m. for the meeting scheduled at 7:00 p.m. Hundreds of American soldiers and airmen were present with their families.

When the invitation was given, an estimated 1,500 walked forward to make decisions for Christ. Some may have been Communists. All of them were people who wanted a new way of life.

Miracle in Germany

NUREMBERG, A CITY WHICH SPAWNED MUCH OF THE NAZI PARTY and witnessed many of Hitler's ponderous power orgies in huge Soldiers' Field, turned out 65,000 strong on a Sunday afternoon to hear an American talk about peace instead of war.

Billy Graham spoke from a platform near the spot from which the German Führer often watched his troops and tanks pass in review.

Americans will remember shots of the scene as Hitler stood on the top balcony, with a swastika waving at his back, and 500,000 soldiers standing at attention in the arena.

Billy didn't speak from the top platform. By choice, he spoke at the foot of a big cross on a level more in line with the people. The marble structure on either side stretched a distance equal to three city blocks. The seats were filled with many of the same Germans who had taken part in the other events.

During the Nazi war games, there were lighted urns of oil at the top of the columns. The urns were without fires for the religious event. A banner underneath each proclaimed "Jesus Christ is the Light of the World."

One German pastor, who had stood on the same field as a storm trooper, said, "The spirit of love was here today. The other time it was a spirit of hate."

Hundreds of American GI's mingled with the gaily dressed Bavarians, some of whom wore the unique leather shorts with shoulder straps.

Shortly before the program was scheduled to begin, the clouds darkened, lightning flashed, and a few drops of rain fell. It appeared that a deluge would sweep over the packed throngs at any minute, but the rain never came.

Something similar had happened the night before in Neckar Stadium at Stuttgart, where 60,000 gathered to hear Billy. When he arose to speak, the wind whipped great clouds of dust across the stadium and it appeared that rain would wash out the proceedings. Billy asked the people to pray that God would hold back the rain. The meeting began and the clouds continued to threaten, but the rain didn't come. Even the disinterested observers noted that rain fell in nearby areas on all sides of the stadium, but none touched the meeting. Ten minutes after the benediction, the rains came down heavily.

"Many people considered this a miracle," Billy commented next day at a press conference.

At the Nuremberg meeting he preached, in the main, the same message that he had used in other European cities.

When he gave the invitation, it was almost impossible for the people to move forward because they were too tightly packed. But they came anyway. The first to step forward was a lady who appeared to be in her seventies. A blonde Aryan youth followed her. Then came scores of others, including GI's in combat boots.

Thousands of Germans and Americans stood there together with Billy, at the foot of the cross.

And they had love in their hearts for one another.

Billy's Interpreter

THE YOUNG GERMAN SOLDIER WAS CAPTURED DURING THE LAST months of World War II and was in a prisoner of war camp.

During his days in action, he had carried a New Testament. But Nazi leaders had taught him to be ashamed of the Book. It had no place in the Germany they planned. In spite of the adverse teaching, however, he read the Testament at every opportunity. There was something different about the words of Jesus. They spoke to his heart.

After his capture he had more time to read. But he was still not willing to read the Book openly. He was reading in bed one night, with the covers pulled up around his head as if asleep. Someone grabbed him by the shoulder and growled, "What are you reading there, soldier?" He held up the Testament and expected a stinging rebuke, or laugh of scorn from his fellow prisoner. Instead, the man said, "I wonder if you would let me read it sometimes."

This man wasn't ashamed. He sat down in the middle of the barracks and read the Testament openly for all to see.

During the next few days the Book was borrowed by other German prisoners. It was a stinging lesson to the young soldier. He determined never again to be ashamed of the gospel of Jesus Christ.

After his release from prison he waited for two years to gain admission to the United States, where he studied at Moody Bible Institute in Chicago.

The same young man stood beside Billy Graham before

over 20,000 in Dortmund's beautiful Westphalia Hall and served as interpreter for the American evangelist.

He had ably filled the same role in several other German cities, where meetings were attended by many thousands of his countrymen. His task as interpreter for the famed preacher has made Wilfried Zibell one of the most promising figures for evangelism in Germany. It is here that he plans to work, telling others about the Bible, a book he was once ashamed to read.

Gracious Queen, Rude Ex-King

ONE OF THE PECULIARITIES OF BILLY GRAHAM'S PHENOMENAL world-wide ministry is that it reaches the queen on her throne, the bum in the gutter, and ordinary individuals in between.

Few men in history have been so blessed with this ability. In recent months the evangelist received invitations from ex-Prime Minister Winston Churchill, President Eisenhower, Queen Elizabeth II, ambassadors, and statesmen. Most of the talks were private, but Billy has revealed that they were Bible-centered. So were the talks he had with a Glasgow taxi driver, a Paris newspaperman, and a German business executive.

His latest invitation from royalty came in Holland from Queen Juliana and Princess Wilhelmina. Princess Wilhelmina, now in her eighties, stepped down from the throne in 1948 after ruling her energetic, friendly people some fifty years. She is regarded by many religious leaders as one devoted to spiritual matters.

Billy and his pretty wife, Ruth, were driven to the magnificent palace at Soestdijk, about thirty-five miles from Amsterdam. They arrived at ten o'clock and were alone with the Queen and Princess until eleven o'clock.

The impressive open door to high places was unceremoniously slammed, however, in one recent instance. It was slammed, ironically, by ex-King Farouk of Egypt, who was tossed out on his royal ear by his own people. The ponderous Farouk, who says he is broke, moved into the same Paris hotel where Billy and his team were staying. Friends of the evangelist thought it would be a wonderful thing if Billy could tell Farouk about the new life offered by Jesus Christ. Billy was willing.

One of the friends knocked on Farouk's door in an effort to make such an arrangement. A cold-faced aide answered the knock and listened stonily to the request. "Just a minute and I will see," said the aide, who left the friend shifting from one foot to the other in the hallway. He came back in a few seconds and said, "King Farouk cannot see Billy Graham." "Will it be possible for them to talk tomorrow?" asked the friend. "King Farouk cannot see Billy Graham tomorrow or anytime," replied the aide.

Sounds of boisterous revelry could be heard from inside the room. Farouk was engaged in his favorite pastime of wine, women, and song. He could not be bothered with the things of God.

Indifferent Norway

BILLY GRAHAM REACHED THE ENTIRE NATION OF NORWAY with one sermon.

The evangelist preached to more than 40,000 in Oslo's Bislet Stadium, with hundreds standing for two hours in an adjoining parking lot and others sitting on rooftops near the fences. Every radio station in Norway broadcast the sermon, with some of the kilocycles spilling over into Russia at northern points.

Forming a small but impressive part of the throng at the stadium were people who came on a special train from the Land of the Midnight Sun, where the little nation links up with Russia. At this time of the year (June), the people there have sunshine twenty-four hours a day. The train originated in the vicinity of Kirkenes, a city located almost as far away from Oslo as Rome, Italy.

Pastors on the train said that a number of people from Russia slipped across the border and made the trip to hear the American preacher. Some of those on board were from the city of Tromso, known as the capital of the Arctic.

One of the local tourist attractions is the German battleship *Tirpitz*, sunk by the RAF in the sound during 1944. Norway was occupied by Germany for five years during World War II, and much of the country was scorched during the retreat, but the people have done a good job of rebuilding their physical assets. The spiritual life of the country has deteriorated badly, however.

A local business leader and member of the committee for the Graham meeting, who gained a measure of fame with heroic resistance work during the Nazi occupation, said churches of Norway were filled during the war. The people relied on God to lead them. As soon as the war was over, he said, the people forgot about God and the churches became practically empty on Sunday.

Religious observers assert that Norway needs a spiritual awakening worse than France.

Books of fact state that almost ninety-six per cent of the population belong to the state Lutheran Church. This sounds wonderful, but the picture is out of focus. Murderers, thieves, and harlots are counted as members of a particular church if they happen to live in the neighborhood.

The people believe in God. They believe in the church. They think the Bible is a good Book. They just don't have time for those things any more. But a small group still believes that God deserves first place in the life of an individual and a nation. It was this group that invited Evangelist Billy Graham for a meeting and the one sermon that spread into every corner of the nation.

He told the people what the Bible has to say about a country that turns its back on God. Hundreds walked out of the stands to make decisions for Christ when the invitation was given, and thousands raised their hands as an indication they were rededicating their lives to God. One of these was an American ambassador.

Some of the indifference had been jolted loose.

Ministers Disagree

THE ONLY ORGANIZED OPPOSITION DURING BILLY'S EUROPEAN Crusade was encountered in Aarhus, Denmark's second largest city.

Eighteen ministers of the state Lutheran Church made public statements in the press and pulpit against Billy and his "modern methods." The same number of ministers lined up in favor of the meeting. The balance was tipped in Billy's favor when Bishop Skat Hoffmeyer came out in favor of the event.

Asked at a press conference for a statement about the eighteen opposing pastors, Billy said:

"Each man is entitled to the freedom of his own opinion. I welcome them to the service and hope they will come with open minds. We have had people oppose us in other places, but many changed their minds after observing our methods and motives.

"The Christian church today has every right to disagree, but we must do it in a spirit of love."

An estimated 10,000 attended the Aarhus meeting. As the service began, an old man, unnoticed by the crowd, dropped to his knees at the rear of the platform and prayed silently for God to bless Billy's efforts. He stayed there and prayed throughout the service.

Scores of people moved from the crowd to the platform during the invitation. The old man looked at them through misty eyes and moved silently away.

His prayers had been answered!

* * *

Short story:

An Oslo man came down to the train when the Graham party left Norway. He said he had been a missionary to Korea and had talked, unsuccessfully, with his own mother and father many times about Christ.

"When Dr. Graham gave the invitation Sunday," he said, "my seventy-three-year-old mother walked onto the field and gave her heart to Christ. She went home, put her arms around the neck of my father, now seventy-five, and told him she had found the Lord. They had prayer together in the home that night for the first time in their lives.

"I believe my father will find Christ soon."

* * *

European random shots:

Ruth Graham spent most of her travel time polishing shoes for herself and other ladies in the party . . . The outstanding follow-up work for all of Billy's campaigns is directed by The Navigators, a Christian organization of men and women who do personal work throughout the world . . . Jerry Beavan, executive secretary for the Graham team, who directs the campaigns, was chuckling one day in Sweden about the American who pulled his long Cadillac into a European service station and said "fill 'er up." He left the motor running. After a while the attendant walked up front and said, "mister, would you mind shutting off the motor, you're getting ahead of me." . . . Jerry's more than capable assistant is Mrs. Betty Lowery, who handles much of the press relations . . . Mr. Willis Haymaker goes into a city well ahead of the Graham team and sets up the meetings. Because of illness, he didn't make the European tour, but was "all over the place" in Scotland.

Big Four Warned

THE BLOODSHOT EYES OF A FRUSTRATED WORLD WERE CENTERED on Geneva, Switzerland.

People around the world wanted peace, and leaders of the Big Four were to begin "talks at the summit" next day. The finest political brains in the world were to be at work.

Another big voice was added to the international discussions in an address on the eve of the Big Four deliberations. Billy Graham, speaking over 800 radio stations, warned the leaders they would accomplish nothing unless God was invited to be the number one delegate. Later in the day he spoke at a mass meeting attended by 20,000. Hundreds of diplomats and newspapermen were present.

In the radio message, he said:

"There is an air of expectancy here in Geneva. The hotels are filled. More than 1,500 newspaper reporters are in town from all over the world to cover this event. Geneva is filled with excitement and confusion. Of all the historic conferences that have been held in this beautiful Swiss city, this is considered the greatest. The Big Four will wrestle with problems that Sir Winston Churchill has said are too great for the human mind to cope with.

"Yesterday I drove out to the house where the Russian delegation is staying. It is heavily guarded and is just as mysterious as the Iron Curtain itself. During the past few weeks the Russians have definitely been showing a new face. They have been making gestures of goodwill toward the

West. Their faces are wreathed in smiles. They've even had some nice things to say about the United States. They're bending over backwards to please the British.

"A number of British pastors have recently toured Russia and have come back with glowing reports of new religious interest. Signs of goodwill and the easing of tension are felt in Geneva on the part of many European observers. However, the majority of American newspapermen and diplomats that I have talked to in the last few hours are convinced that the West is being deceived and that Russia is presenting a false face in order to hide her real intentions.

"One newspaperman went so far as to say that all of this goodwill is the prelude to an all-out devastating guided missile attack against the United States at any moment. He points out that the Japanese caught us being lulled to sleep by the smiling, bowing Japanese diplomats on the day of Pearl Harbor. He says that Russia now has the capability of destroying most of the United States within the space of a few hours. On the other hand, another newspaperman says he believes the tremendous economic and military power of the West has now made the Communists re-think their whole position and that they're ready to sue for peace and relax the cold war.

"This gives you an idea of the extreme caution and fear on the one hand and the extreme optimism and hope on the other that is felt in Geneva.

"Certainly every American should be praying that God will give to President Eisenhower supernatural wisdom and superhuman ability. May I say this personal word. I believe that he has come to Geneva with a great sense of responsibility and with a dependence on God for help.

"This conference in Geneva has been called a Summit Conference, insofar as human ability is concerned. The one cry in Geneva is peace. Some people are ready to sell their soul and conscience for even a temporary peace.

'I have asked many people here, 'How can you have a summit conference and how can you hope for peace without the Prince of peace?'

"In all the pre-conference meetings at Geneva I have hardly heard God mentioned. Everything is being done on a humanistic level. Christ is forgotten. There is little time for God. There have been other peace conferences in history where God was forgotten and Christ was left out that have ended in war and disaster.

"Tonight in Geneva we are having a gigantic meeting. Thousands of people will gather. We are going to do our best to insert Christ into this conference. Outstanding clergymen and diplomats will be present. We are praying that it will set a spiritual stage and a recognition of God in the affairs of men for this Big Four Conference.

"During my message I shall remind them of summit meetings in the Bible. First, there was the meeting of Moses with God on Mount Sinai. Here God gave to Moses the Ten Commandments. The Bible teaches that God is a holy and righteous God. The Ten Commandments were an expression of God's righteousness and purity. These were the standards by which men were to live.

"God told the people, 'If ye break these commandments ye shall surely die.'

"What a conference that must have been. Moses, tall and stalwart, taking his shoes off, standing in humility on holy ground, talking face to face with his Creator. This was a true summit meeting, God and man discussing the problems of the human race together and God giving Moses the ten rules of human behavior.

"If only the Big Four leaders in Geneva could realize that all of their problems stem from one basic problem, which is the sin of human nature. The problems of the world are not economic or political; they are spiritual.

"We continue to wrestle with the problems of human

iniquity and human failure. Nations have reached agreements only to have them broken time after time.

"Why? Because they were building their hopes and agreements on the cracked and sinking foundation of human nature. For thousands of years men have failed to take into account the human equation. These so-called peace agreements are no stronger than human nature and all men are sinners by nature and have the capacity of breaking any and all agreements.

"Where are the agreements of Teheran and Yalta? They have been broken long ago and little nations that looked with such hope to those summit meetings ten years ago have been disillusioned.

"Why? Because they were reached without taking the human equation into consideration. The men who made the agreements and who have broken them are not altogether to blame. We are all guilty and we've all broken God's laws and God says the result of our transgression is death.

"There was another summit meeting of history that offers to the world its only ultimate hope at this moment. It was the greatest peace conference of all time.

"In every church in Europe there is a cross. The cross has become the symbol of Christianity. Why? Because it was on the cross that the foundation of man's reconciliation to God was made. The only cure for sin lies at the foot of that cross. The ultimate possibility of lifting human nature to the place where it will love instead of hate and will practice honesty instead of deceit and will keep its agreements with integrity is found only at the foot of this cross.

"The reason we do not have peace in the world is that we do not have peace in our souls. There can be no peace in the hearts of men without a reconciliation to God. All men who will pay the price of repentance and receive Christ by faith can have a new nature and a new heart. We can never build a better world until we have better men and the only way men can be made better is by the transforming and re-generating power of Christ.

"Last, there is a summit conference yet to come. It will be the greatest conference of all time. History is rushing madly toward this supreme moment. The Bible teaches it from Genesis to Revelation. It is the greatest fact of the universe. This summit meeting offers hope to millions and if they only knew it, despair and judgment to millions more. This meeting will take place in the air when Christ returns for His own.

"I have found here in Europe that theologians and ministers of all denominations are begining to preach and teach the second coming of Jesus Christ. It is a theme that I have found discussed from one end of Europe to the other. There is more talk on this side of the Atlantic concerning the coming again of Christ than at possibly any time in recent church history.

"The Bible definitely teaches that Christ is coming back to this earth again. To all those who have received Him it will mean a thrilling and triumphal moment. To those who have rejected Him it will mean judgment and banishment from His kingdom, because the human race has largely rejected the peace that Christ made for us at Calvary. Our great hope now lies in the coming again of Christ as the conference gets under way here in Geneva.

"It is my deepest conviction that Christ is our only hope. This Geneva conference may give some temporary hope and issue some high-sounding words of encouragement, but basically the issues between light and darkness have not changed, and the only ultimate way that it will be completely dispelled is when Christ returns again."

The President Prays

PRESIDENT DWIGHT EISENHOWER, THE MAN WHO REPRESENTED the United States at the most prayed-for peace conference in history, had some rare qualifications for the task—the cold-blooded intelligence of an Army general who was not ashamed to kneel in humility before his God.

Such a combination was unbeatable at the Big Four talks.

The realistic general, who has known the horrors of war, did not make concessions with the lives of people just to get a Russian signature on a piece of paper. But the man of simple faith, who believes that God is still in control of the world's destiny, prayerfully sought agreements not believed possible.

President Eisenhower has seen young fathers die in the filth of muddy ditches. He has seen innocent children with their legs and arms blown away. And he has seen the quiet, peaceful beauty of a farm in America, where food grows from the good earth and people are free to live and dream dreams.

Such a man was not awed by the likes of Bulganin and Khrushchev.

The President's face, on the Sunday before the conference was to begin on Monday, mirrored the serious attitude with which he faced the difficult talks.

Together with his entire delegation of immediate advisers he attended the American Church (Episcopal) in Geneva. The church was small. Most crossroad villages in

America have larger ones. It had a capacity of about 150 and each person who entered was screened by the U. S. Secret Service. There were no holes in the screen.

President Eisenhower sat with his wife, Secretary of State Dulles, Undersecretary Herbert Hoover, Jr., and other advisers. Sitting diagonally behind the President were Billy Graham and Cliff Barrows. Some fifty newspapermen filled other pews.

Faced with such a congregation, the Rev. Gerald B. O'Grady didn't appear a bit nervous, but the pulpit may have shielded a little knee shaking. He preached a gospel sermon in which he told how God used faithful men to carry out His plans. The President and congregation knelt in prayer, asking God's blessing on efforts of the Big Four. Before leaving home the chief of state had asked all Americans to be in their churches to pray for peace.

One of the most enjoyable points of the service to President Eisenhower, evidenced by his rapt look of attention, came when a Negro woman sang "Sweet Little Jesus Boy."

In making the church anouncements, the Rev. O'Grady reminded the congregation that Dr. Billy Graham was having a city-wide rally at 5:00 p.m. in Eaux Vives Park. Mrs. Eisenhower leaned over and whispered something to the President when the announcement was made. They did not attend the rally. Another engagement conflicted.

The Graham meeting developed into more than a city-wide effort. Among the estimated 20,000 who turned out were scores from France, Italy, Germany, and other nearby countries. Thousands of them sat on the grass in the warm sunshine. Cars bearing United Nations tags were spotted on the outskirts. A member of the Russian delegation had informed a press reporter that some of the Soviet representatives would be present. Reporters from throughout the world were seated at the press table.

In his preliminary remarks before delivering the message, Billy said:

"The next few days in Geneva could determine the destiny of the world. Hopes and dreams of people everywhere are centered on this city. The leaders have warned us not to expect too much in the way of results, but the people do expect much. They look at the stockpile of weapons capable of destroying civilization and ask that the leaders forget their personal ambitions and national dreams and turn in humility to Almighty God.

"We have taken counsel with each other; now let us counsel with God. In His mercy and love He is giving the world one more chance."

Billy then prayed for each one of the Big Four by name. He reminded the people it was their duty to pray for the men. God's conditions for peace, he said, were that nations humble themselves, pray, repent of sin, and turn to Him in faith.

After the conclusion of his message, Billy gave an invitation for people to surrender their lives to Christ. Several hundred did.

The men, women, and young people were quieter than usual as they walked slowly from the park. They were thinking about the four men who would sit down around a table and decide their destiny.

Thousands of them were hoping that God would be sitting at the head of the table.

Impact on World

BILLY GRAHAM, WHO WORE THE MANTLE OF AMERICA'S "favorite son" with dignity in the palaces of queens and the kitchens of slum houses, returned to the United States after five months abroad.

During those months he addressed over 4,000,000 people and persuaded over 100,000 of them that "Jesus Christ is the way, the truth, and the life." No other preacher in history has approached such a figure in a comparable time.

Major spiritual awakenings that could change the course of history have taken place in Scotland, England, and Germany. Seeds of moral rearmament have been planted in France, Switzerland, Holland, and the Scandinavian countries. News of the unusual religious renaissance has been taken behind the Iron Curtain of Russia by people who risked their lives to hear a young man talk about old truths.

The clergy in several countries has been revitalized. Ministers who had grown discouraged in the face of mass indifference are now preaching with authority and simplicity. Their people are responding.

Unnumbered millions have listened to Billy by radio and television.

Climax of the long overseas stay came when Billy spoke at a rally in Geneva on the eve of the historic Big Four peace conference. Geneva, however, was just the climax in a series of climaxes.

Many things stand out in looking back over the months

abroad—the old gentleman from New Orleans who saved his money for two years in order to visit Scotland, where he could "pray for Billy and witness for Christ" . . . a giant Highlander, who came down out of the hills because he heard people were finding God in Glasgow . . . separated husband and wife finding each other in counseling room after both had made decisions for Christ . . . Sir John Hunt, conqueror of Mt. Everest, standing on turf of Wembley Stadium with rain running down his face as he turned to the Creator of the mountains . . . art student finding Christ in Paris on night he had planned suicide in Seine River . . . people sitting in trees to hear message at Zurich . . . private audience in Holland with Queen Juliana and Princess Wilhelmina . . . same in England with Queen Elizabeth . . . rain falling on all sides of stadium at Stuttgart but not a drop inside until ten minutes after meeting . . . Germans and Americans standing before cross in Nuremberg, where Hitler stood before Swastika and watched Nazi legions march . . . cripple walking five miles on crutches to attend meeting at Frankfurt . . . aged man hidden behind platform as he knelt in prayer during entire meeting in Denmark.

The foreign correspondent of a Chicago daily, sitting next to me on a plane in Germany one day, asked: "What in the world do you find to write about? Doesn't Billy Graham say just about the same thing everywhere he goes?"

The message is the same, but it reaches a thousand lives in a thousand different ways. Every one of them is a story. And then, there are the tragic stories of people who live for the present, ignore the future, and curse the past.

Billy Graham has made an impact on the world, from presidents and royalty to taxi drivers and businessmen. A number of America's leading writers have commented on the impact in recent months.

They have stated in print that the thirty-seven-year-old

evangelist from Montreat, N. C., has done more for the United States abroad than all the politicians rolled into one.

And he has done it with the world's oldest message!

Billy Comes Home

THE PROUD MOTHER AND FATHER BEAMED!

Mr. and Mrs. Frank Graham were not proud solely because their son, Billy, was world famous. They were proud because he was home after a long time away.

He was home on the farm near Charlotte, N. C., where he had spent his boyhood.

And sometimes during the first day his six feet two inches were stretched out full length on a rug in the living room.

"It is his favorite place to relax," said Mrs. Graham. "All during his boyhood, Billy Frank would stretch out there, and he still does whenever he manages to get home."

Mrs. Graham made it a point to have some ripe tomatoes in the kitchen and some salt nearby. Billy had gone into the house hundreds of times, grabbed a whole tomato, and eaten it with salt. Mothers have a way of remembering things that please their children.

Billy isn't given special treatment at home. With two sisters and one brother, all grown, he is just one of the family.

"Sometimes I think his brother, Melvin, might have made a better preacher," laughed Mrs. Graham. Melvin looks after the dairy farm, which is still in the family.

Mr. and Mrs. Graham have a home where there is laughter and love in abundance. They began the home on a solid foundation. On the first night of their honeymoon they knelt in the hotel room and dedicated their family to God. Billy is the older son.

Millions of Americans, Britons, and Europeans who have heard the energetic, fast-talking evangelist will not begrudge him the catnap on the rug. No person ever deserved one more. But a catnap it was. Billy had to move on quickly to his own family and home at Montreat, N. C.

Even this reunion was all too brief. He was committed to numerous speaking engagements around the country.

Scores of admirers were at the dock in New York when Billy returned aboard the sleek ocean liner, the *United States*. He didn't tarry long in the big city. A few hours later he was on the train for Washington, D. C.

The following afternoon he did something no other preacher had done for forty-seven years. He was invited to address over 350 newspapermen at the National Press Club. A number of Congressmen were present as special guests. Secretaries and office workers crowded into doorways and filled the balcony.

Club officials had discussed closing the bar for the occasion, but decided to leave it open. Billy's first stop inside was the bar. He ordered a glass of milk.

He delivered a hard-hitting address on what had been done abroad, how it had been done, and why. In the process he gave the distinguished writers the gospel of Christ and told them "you must be born again to enter the Kingdom of Heaven."

Billy appealed to the newspapermen to exert their vast influence for God.

"There is enough power in this room to shake the world," he said.

A rather old gentleman approached him after the conclusion of the address and said:

"Billy, I am a retired newspaperman who has been attending these meetings for years. We have never had a speech like the one you just made."

Another writer remarked with astonishment as he walked to the elevators:

"This is the first time I have ever forgotten to look at my watch during a talk."

"Never saw the fellows listen so hard," said another.

On Sunday morning Billy spoke at the National Presbyterian Church, where President and Mrs. Eisenhower are members. The President was away on this particular Sunday. He has heard the evangelist speak at his church on other occasions, however.

That night Billy was on a nationwide television hookup, making his second appearance in less than a year on "Meet the Press."

He left shortly after the interview by train for Charlotte.

The next big moment in his busy life came when he reached Montreat, where he was joyously greeted by his wife and four children. Ruth, who had accompanied him on part of the European tour, had returned home two months earlier. They have three little girls and one boy.

The children are unaware of the fact that their father is a famous preacher. They are aware of the fact that he stays away too long and that they miss him terribly.

One of the biggest prices Billy pays for his ministry is having to stay away about eleven months of the year from the family he loves.

He received a letter one day in Paris, shortly before he was to sail, and when he opened it the picture of a small boy fell out.

Billy glanced at the picture and exclaimed, "Who in the world would be sending me a picture of their boy?"

He was about to toss the picture on a table when he suddenly took a closer look.

"That's my son," he yelled as he recognized little three-year-old Franklin.

It was time to come home!

Crusade Statistics

	Glasgow
Attendance, six weeks	2,647,000
Decisions	52,523
	London
Attendance, eight services	500,000
Decisions	25,000
	Paris
Attendance, six services	45,000
Decisions	2,000
	Zurich
Attendance, one service	50,000
Decisions	5,000
	Geneva
Attendance, two services	40,000
Decisions	3,000
	U. S. Service Bases
Attendance	25,000
Decisions	7,000
	Mannheim
Attendance, one service	40,000
Decisions	1,500
	Stuttgart
Attendance, one service	60,000
Decisions	2,400
	Nuremberg
Attendance, one service	65,000
Decisions	2,500
	Dortmund
Attendance, one service	30,000
Decisions	1,800

	Frankfurt
Attendance, one service	40,000
Decisions	2,000
	Rotterdam
Attendance, one service	65,000
Decisions	2,000
	Oslo
Attendance, two services	77,000
Decisions	1,000
	Gothenburg, Sweden
Attendance, one service	26,000
Decisions	150
	Aarhus, Denmark
Attendance, one service	10,000
Decisions	200
	Total Attendance
	3,720,000
	Total Decisions
	125,350

(An estimated 75,000,000 looked and listened to Billy Graham on television and radio. About 100,000 others made decisions through these mediums.)